Heritage Pub Walks in the Isle of Man

Heritage Pub Walks in the Isle of Man

Ann Reeder

authorHOUSE®

AuthorHouse™
1663 Liberty Drive
Bloomington, IN 47403
www.authorhouse.com
Phone: 1-800-839-8640

© 2011 by Ann Reeder. All rights reserved.

No part of this book may be reproduced, stored in a retrieval system, or transmitted by any means without the written permission of the author.

The moral rights of the author have been asserted.

Author's note: Every effort has been made to provide accurate information about the routes, pubs, heritage sites and facilities. However, details may change over time. We are sorry if you find any inaccuracies and would welcome information from readers and users so that we can update future editions; email ann@frontline-communications.co.uk

To plan your visit, see www.gov.im/tourism

First published by AuthorHouse   11 May 2011

ISBN: 978-1-4567-7824-8 (sc)

Printed in the United States of America

This book is printed on acid-free paper.

Because of the dynamic nature of the Internet, any web addresses or links contained in this book may have changed since publication and may no longer be valid. The views expressed in this work are solely those of the author and do not necessarily reflect the views of the publisher, and the publisher hereby disclaims any responsibility for them.

Photographs and maps: Tim Daniel

Contents

Location map of pub walks and heritage
   sites in the Isle of Man xi

Introduction xiii

Manx real ale and brewing xvii

Manx heritage xix

Walking in Mann xxiii

Introduction to the heritage pub walks xxv

Walk 1 Douglas—the capital
   The Woodbourne Hotel and the Manx Museum 1
   The walk (Easy; 3.5 miles; half day) 3

Walk 2 Peel—the sunset city
   The Creek Inn and the House of
      Manannan and Peel Castle 8
   The walk (Medium; 4 miles; full day) 11

Walk 3 Castletown—the ancient capital
   The Sidings Inn and the Nautical Museum,
      Castle Rushen, the Old House of Keys
      and the Old Grammar School 17
   The walk (Easy; 4.5 miles, plus optional
      extra 3 miles; full day) 21

Walk 4 Tynwald—Parliamentary ceremonial
   The White House Hotel and Tynwald Hill
      at St Johns, along the Heritage Trail 28
   The walk (Medium; 7 miles; half day) 31

Walk 5 Laxey—the Lady Isabella
   The Shore Hotel and the Laxey Wheel
      and Mines 35
   The walk (Medium; 3.5 miles; half day) 37

Walk 6 Ramsey—'down the north'
   The Trafalgar Hotel and the Grove Museum 41
   The walk (Easy; 4 miles; half day) 43

Walk 7 Port St Mary—crofters' settlement
   The Albert Hotel and Cregneash 47
   The walk (More challenging; shorter walk
      5 miles; longer walk 8 miles; full day) 49

Walk 8 Port Erin—seaside elegance
   The Bay Hotel and the Steam Railway Museum 57
   The walk (More challenging; 5 miles; half day) 59

Walk 9 Douglas—the age of the Victorians
   The Rovers Return pub and Marine Drive
      and a ride on the steam railway 65
   The walk (Medium; 5 miles; plus possible
      3 miles back if the steam railway is not
      running; half day) 68

'Walk' 10 The final lap—the tour of the
motorcycles and the view from the top
The Sulby Glen Hotel, the TT course
and a short ascent of Snaefell................................. 73
The walk (Medium; less than two miles;
30 minutes ascent and 20 minutes descent).......... 76

Useful contacts and information.................................... 84

Thanks to my Manx friends for introducing me to this wonderful island, and to Tim, my parents Eric and Margaret, family and friends for accompanying me on many of these walks and for joining me on visits to the Story of Mann.

Location map of pub walks and heritage sites in the Isle of Man

Snaefell

'Walk' 10 – The final lap
The Sulby Glen Hotel and Snaefell

Walk 6. The Trafalgar Hotel, Ramsey

Tynwald Hill, St Johns

Walk 5 – The Shore Hotel, Laxey

Walk 2 – The Creek Inn, Peel

Walk 1. The Woodbourne Hotel, Douglas

Walk 4 – The White House, Peel

Niarbyl

Walk 9 – The Rovers Return, Douglas

Walk 8. The Bay Hotel, Port Erin

Walk 7. The Albert Hotel, Port St Mary

Walk 3. The Sidings Inn, Castletown

Story of Mann sites visited on particular walks

Castle Rushen (walk 3)
Cregneash (walk 7)
The Grove Museum (walk 6)
House of Manannan (walk 2)
The Lady Isabella or Laxey Wheel (walk 5)
Manx Museum (walk 1)
The Nautical Museum (walk 3)
Niarbyl café and Visitor Centre (after 'walk' 10)
The Old Grammar School (walk 3)
The Old House of Keys (walk 3)
Peel Castle (walk 2)
Rushen Abbey (extension on walk 3)

Introduction

The Isle of Man (Mann) may be best known for the TT (Tourist Trophy) motorcycle races and it is true that the island is awash with gleaming machines in early June each year. But there are many other aspects of the island, which draw visitors time and again—its history, its culture, its scenery and its welcome.

While it would be an error to compare the incomparable Isle of Man with England, Scotland, Wales or Ireland, Mann presents the very best of many of their attractive landscapes in miniature. It's a glittering kaleidoscope of hills, valleys, rugged coastline, sandy bays, glens and streams—with the sea never far from view. Its romantic Manx Gaelic name, Ellan Vannin, captures the moods and beauty of the island, just 33 miles by 13 miles at its extremes.

The island cherishes its independence and enjoys its own Parliament (the Tynwald, which has been in continuous existence for over 1,000 years), currency, stamps, flag (red with the three legs symbol) and language, and its status as a Crown dependency.

The Isle of Man is a good place to relax. Indeed, there is a Manx saying "traa-dy-liooar", meaning "there's time enough", which is a very welcome motto for a holiday. Visitors can enjoy quiet drives among wild and unspoilt scenery, along the coast or over the moors. Secluded and peaceful glens provide a gentle stroll away from it all. There are wide expanses of sand or rocky coves disturbed only by seals or seagulls and many uncluttered golf courses set amidst delightful scenery.

The island is a treasure house for the historian, throwing up everywhere reminders of its Celtic and Norse heritage, the troubled years of English and Scottish rule, and more recently the Victorians' influence on its economy (mining), transport and tourism. Changing times and changing weather are recorded in the many intriguing ruins scattered the length and breadth of the island. The strong sense of history enables visitors to feel away from it all—an important quality today.

Getting around is very easy. You can take your car or hire one, or use the well-connected bus service. Or you can travel from south to north on a century old heritage transport network using the steam railway from Port Erin to Douglas and the electric tram from Douglas to Ramsey, connecting steam and electric in Douglas by the nostalgic horse-drawn tram. An Explorer ticket is excellent value giving flexible options for your length of stay. And, of course, the island is excellent for walking.

This book is designed to give you a flavour of the Island, day by day. It features some outstanding walks for a range of abilities and time, introduces you to the main heritage sites of Mann and invites you to relax after the walk at a welcoming pub. Many of the pubs on the island have delightful settings overlooking the sea, glens or harbours; the selection in this book all serve real ale, often quality local food and are close to a site of the Story of Mann.

Heritage Pub Walks in the Isle of Man

I have enjoyed preparing this collection with family and friends, and hope you enjoy your stay. Whatever you choose to do and wherever you visit, you will be delighted by what Mann has to offer. It's a place that you will want to visit again.

Manx real ale and brewing

In 2010 the Island played host to the annual members' weekend and AGM of CAMRA, the campaign for real ale, an appropriate location given the Island's brewing heritage. Members enjoyed not only the usual beer tastings, but visits to the outstanding range of pubs and tours of three of the Island's breweries.

The Isle of Man has a long tradition of brewing and over five centuries has had an impressive range of breweries and drinking establishments. In 1793, for example, it had 18 breweries. The Island has a high ratio of pubs to people and quite recently, it is claimed, there was a pub for every 500 residents or 1.5 pubs per square mile!

Manx beer must be produced to the strict Pure Beer Act 1874 that made it unlawful to use additives and chemicals in the brewing process. Only hops, malt, water, yeast and sugar is allowed, though an amendment was passed in 1999 which permitted the use of specific additives such as fruit (and to allow Okells to use three spices in its Eastern Spice beer).

"No brewer shall use in the brewing, making, mixing with, recovering or colouring, any beer, or any liquid made to resemble beer, or have in his possession any copperas, coculus Indicus, nux vomica, grains of paradise, Guinea pepper, or opium, or any article, ingredient, or preparation whatever, for, or as a substitute for, malt or sugar or hops."

Isle of Man Pure Beer Act 1874

Ann Reeder

You can visit three breweries on the Island on organised tours: the oldest in existence, Okells; Bushy's that started out as a brew pub, and a micro-brewery, the Old Laxey Brewing Company. All have one or more tied houses and supply a range of pubs on the island.

Dr Wiliam Okell founded Okells Falcon Brewery on Castle Hill in Douglas in 1850. In 1986, Okells took over the Castletown Brewery, which had been brewing since the 1760s and even as early as the 1500s. The former Castletown Brewery buildings by the inner harbour have been converted into flats. Okells is the main brewery on the Island and now operates from a hi-tech brewery in Kewaigue on the outskirts of Douglas, which it built in 1994. Tours are conducted by appointment—see www.okells.co.uk, telephone 01624 699400 or email mac@okells.co.uk. The core beers are Okells Bitter, Okells Mild, Maclir (after the Manx Celtic legend, the sea god Manannan Mac Lir) and Doctor Okells IPA, and there are seasonal beers and specials.

Bushy's expanded from its origin as a home brew pub in Douglas in 1986 to its Mount Murray brewery in Santon, south of Douglas in 1990. Its core beers are Ruby Mild, Bushy's Export Bitter, Old Bushy Tail and Castletown Bitter. Tours are by arrangement; visit www.bushys.com, telephone 01624 661244 or email bushy@manx.net.

The Old Laxey Brewing Company supplies its Bosun Bitter to the Shore Hotel in Laxey, its tied house next door to the microbrewery. Tours are by arrangement; telephone 01624 863214 or email shore@mcb.net.

Manx heritage

The outstanding heritage trail, the multi-sited Story of Mann, is one of the best collections of museums or 'cultural landscapes' in the world. Winning many awards, the Story of Mann charts 10,000 years of history of the island in ways that all ages can enjoy—from the attractive social history displays at the Manx Museum, through the state of the art House of Manannan in Peel, to the jumble of cottages, workshops and working farmland at the crofters' and fishermen's settlement at Cregneash.

There can't be such a range of preserved transport within such a small space as on the Isle of Man—over 40 miles of heritage track from the late nineteenth century and still working. The steam railway has operated since 1873 and still runs the fifteen and a half miles from Douglas to Port Erin from Easter to October and at other times for occasional specials, while the Manx Electric Railway opened in 1893 and still runs from Douglas to Ramsey via Laxey. The Snaefell Mountain Railway takes 30 minutes to climb the four and a half miles from Laxey to the summit of Snaefell at 2,036 feet, managing a gradient of 1 in 12. It took only seven months to build, opening in 1895, and still delights visitors with outstanding views and a unique experience, travelling in original passenger cars. Linking steam and electric are the horse-drawn trams that clatter along Douglas Promenade from the Sea Terminal to the Terminus at Summer Hill throughout the summer season—look out for designated alighting and boarding points. The system opened in 1876 to transport holiday-makers to their hotel from the steam packet sea terminal. This network of vintage transport not only evokes the Victorian heyday of tourism, but will enable you to enjoy many of the walks in this book.

Sites recently have been excavated at Ronaldsway airport and Rushen Abbey, whilst St Patrick's Isle off the causeway at Peel has yielded artefacts and reveals ruins indicating it to be one of the most important heritage sites on the island. At Balladoole in the south, a Viking ship burial was discovered, dating from prehistoric times. South Barrule is a hill fort, possibly from the late Bronze Age. Cashtal Yn Ard in Maughold and King Orry's grave, near Laxey are chambered tombs, and another stone circle, Mull or Meayll Hill outside Cregneash, was probably used for rituals and burials centuries ago.

Other religious sites include the ruins on St Patrick's Isle and on St Michael's Island, Lonan Old Church, Maughold Church and St German's cathedral in Peel, as well as the many keeils (chapels) across the island and the stone crosses that feature particularly in Maughold, Andreas and Braddan.

Industrial sites are in evidence in the chimneys of deserted mines, quarry workings and the empty cases of waterwheels and mills across the island.

Mann's social history is well-described in tableaux at the Manx Museum, throughout the Story of Mann and through the evident legacy of Victorian tourism, whilst the revival of the Manx language is demonstrated on road signs, school names and at the popular annual folk festival Yn Cruinnacht.

Heritage Pub Walks in the Isle of Man

The history of the TT is displayed at the Manx Museum, there are memorabilia around the island and you can follow the course, noting the milestones and incredible corners along the way. Details on the TT at http://www.iomtt.com and on the Story of Mann at www.gov.im/mnh

This book of walks invites you to visit a significant selection of the heritage sites that the Isle of Man has to offer those interested in the past. Their imaginative presentation through the Story of Mann especially brings the past to life and makes it accessible and interesting to all ages.

Walking in Mann

The Isle of Man is an all-year round attraction for walkers, and has a delightful range of scenery in which to walk—sweeping expanses of sandy bays and rocky coastline, challenging cliff top paths and hills, secluded shady glens, unspoilt windswept hillsides and moorland, and fascinating town trails within the main attractive and heritage laden settlements.

The 227 square miles of Mann contain at least 300 footpaths, including three long distance paths. Much of the island is wild unspoilt hill, glen and moorland, so you can walk without meeting other people and can keep away from the noise and fumes of traffic.

The long-distance footpaths are the Raad ny Foillan ('Way of the Gull'), that takes you 95 miles around the amazing coastline; the Millennium Way that is based on the Royal Way (first recorded in the 1300s) and runs 26 miles from Sky Hill outside Ramsey (the site of a victory by King Orry over the Manx in 1079) to Castletown over the northern hills through the central valley and along the river to the harbour; and the Bayr ny Skeddan, the Herring Road, following the historic route of the fishing folk carrying herring landed at Peel through to the port at Castletown, 14 miles away.

The island has a backbone of inviting hills extending from the north east to the south west which make for relatively easy ascent and offer wide-ranging views over the island, often from coast to coast with the sea never far from view.

The coastal scenery is breath-taking. The island is located in the midst of the Irish Sea so offers marvellous views across to the hills and mountains of neighbours, the United Kingdom and Ireland, just 26 miles away at the nearest point. The rugged coastline of the south and south west of the island and across the Calf of Man offer more challenging climbs and beautiful views along the sea, while the gentle sands 'down the north' offer sweeping vistas and easy strolls.

There are seventeen national glens on the island—mountain and coastal glens. There are no admission charges and they generally provide for pastoral strolls. They range from Summerhill Glen in Douglas through the popular Silverdale Glen with its water-powered roundabout and boating lake, through the well-trodden Glen Helen to the more remote Glen Mooar and the steep track beside a waterfall, down to the sea, in the Dhoon. A few feature cafés or restaurants such as Glen Helen; some have disabled access, others are more challenging. Groudle Glen has a miniature railway. Many run down to the sea, such as the delightful Glen Maye on the west coast of the island.

Twelve 'Warden's Walks' have been devised by the Government's Forestry Warden, ranging from an easy walk of an hour to a strenuous hiker's trail taking up to seven hours, and there are nature trails at the Ayres and Scarlett. Heritage and/or maritime trails are marked in the major towns of Douglas, Ramsey, Castletown and Peel, and there is the ten and a half mile route of the disused steam railway line from Douglas to Peel. So something for everyone!

Introduction to the heritage pub walks

The walks in this book are circular, accessible by public transport, feature visits to significant Manx heritage sites and include a place for Manx refreshment.

If you travel to the walks by public transport, you can experience the classic heritage routes of the Horse Tram, the Manx Electric Railway and the Isle of Man Steam Railway or use the excellent network of buses; up to date timetables are available at www.iombusandrail.info

The sequence of the walks provides the ideal introduction to the island. The walks are generally in the chronological order of Manx history and cover all of the major towns and heritage sites.

There are admission charges to some of the Story of Mann sites, so it would be worthwhile to purchase multi-site saver tickets (the five site seasonal pass or the ten day heritage explorer pass). Members of the National Trust, English Heritage, the Museum Association and the International Council of Museums benefit from a reciprocal arrangement with Manx National Heritage, which provides free or discounted admission on production of a valid membership card at the Story of Mann site. Details at http://www.gov.im/mnh/information/

Our starting point for the sequence of walks is Douglas and a visit to the Manx Museum so that you can watch an outstanding film of the story of Mann before you venture further.

Ann Reeder

Having watched Mann's history unfold on the large screen you will have been captivated by the legends and the atmosphere of this island of treasures. Now you will be able to explore many of the sites of the island's history for yourself by following the subsequent walks in this book.

As a day-time finale, the tenth section includes a short walk that takes you to the summit of Snaefell, the highest mountain on the island. There, you can take in the breath-taking views of the island and the surrounding coastlines and hills before you leave. This walk is part of a tour that provides an opportunity for you to drive a lap of the historic and world renowned TT course (albeit at sensible speeds!) and to enjoy the outstanding scenery on a last overall look at Mann.

Then for a meal at the end of your walks, book the upstairs table in the window at the Niarbyl Café and Visitor Centre on the beautiful west coast. First, sit by the rocks at the shoreline to relax and reflect on this special place, then enjoy a meal above this outstanding coastline as the sun sets over the Irish Sea. See http://www.gov.im/mnh/heritage/restaurants for details and opening hours, and make sure you book ahead on 01624 843300. At Niarbyl you might recognise a film location for Waking Ned (one of many recent films made in the Isle of Man), spot the fin of a basking shark in the water and feel exhilarated by the rocky coastline and cliffs of this awe-inspiring and beautiful south west coast.

There is so much to discover in the Isle of Man. I hope that this book provides you with an overview of the significant sites of Mann's heritage, a range of beautiful walks in historic,

Heritage Pub Walks in the Isle of Man

attractive or interesting settings, and an opportunity to relax over a Manx beer. Make sure you take "time enough" to enjoy a slower pace of life in an island that breathes out its history and inspires you to return.

Walk 1 Douglas—the capital

The Woodbourne Hotel and the Manx Museum

Address: The Woodbourne Hotel, Alexander Drive, Douglas IM2 3QF
Tel: 01624 676754
Website: www.manngo.im
Hours: Monday to Friday from 2 pm until midnight and Saturday and Sunday from noon until midnight. Hours may vary at bank holidays, Christmas and during the TT and Manx Grand Prix.

Real ale:	Okells Mild, Red and Alt and seasonal beers, plus regularly changing UK guests and seasonal beers, including Stonehenge Sign of Spring
Food:	Not available
Parking:	On-street parking or Chester Street public car park

This is a striking Gothic looking Victorian built popular and friendly local with no frills. It has a lounge, a 'Gentlemen's bar' and a vaults bar. Large screens show football matches, including 3 pm kick-offs. There is a pool table, a quiz every Sunday and an 'open mic' night once a month. There is a covered non-smoking area at the rear, but no seating or garden.

Opposite the pub, between Queen's Avenue and Queen's Terrace, is the Douglas Corporation Centenary Garden, redeveloped in 1996 to celebrate the centenary of the Corporation, the local government of the town.

Manx heritage

Address:	Manx Museum
Hours:	All year from Monday to Saturday from 10 am to 5 pm, except Christmas Day, Boxing Day and New Year's Day
Charge:	Free admission
Catering:	Bayroom restaurant
Shop:	Manx heritage shop for postcards, gifts, books, jewellery etc
Parking:	Limited on-site for disabled drivers; Chester Street car park

Heritage Pub Walks in the Isle of Man

Any visit to the Isle of Man should start with the short film at the museum. It is an excellent introduction to the island, as it atmospherically conjures up the history of Mann. It sets the scene and introduces you to the island's legends, history, culture and traditions. The Museum contains cased artefacts from early history in the Prehistoric Archaeology Gallery, the Viking Gallery and a natural history gallery. There is a map gallery, the national art gallery and two excellent social history galleries covering the TT (Tourist Trophy) races, tourism, the finance sector and the 'voice of the people'. A restaurant and a heritage shop are located at the Museum, which also is home to the Manx National Archive.

The walk (Easy; 3.5 miles; half day)

Although this begins in a residential area, it is a varied and scenic walk. You cross Noble's Park, pass the Grandstand of the TT circuit and descend through Summerhill Glen, before taking in a length of the Promenade along the wide sweep of Douglas Bay.

WALK 1

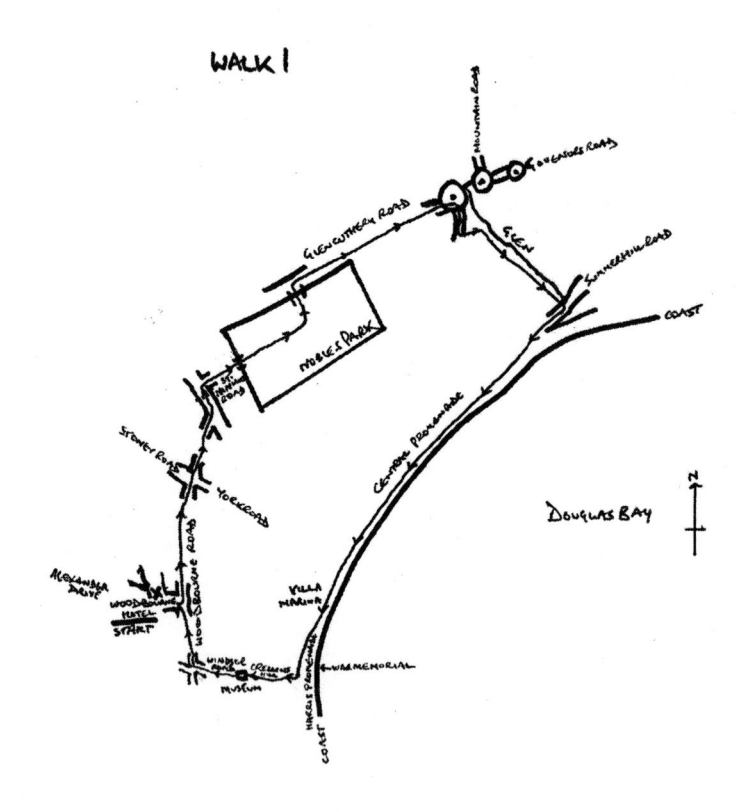

Heritage Pub Walks in the Isle of Man

Turn left outside the Woodbourne Hotel (the 'Woody') down Alexander Drive to reach Woodbourne Road. Turn left and continue ahead crossing York Road at traffic lights. Turn left into Ballaquayle Road, and soon after turn right into St Ninian's Road. Soon you will enter Noble's Park.

Do not turn towards the bandstand to cross the park immediately, but continue ahead keeping the pavilion on your left. The Grandstand, the start and finish of the TT and Manx Grand Prix course, will be visible; (fans sitting there on race days can watch motorcyclists pass at over 150 mph!)

Take the footpath lined with ornate lamp columns bearing the three legs of Mann and keep left of the green fence that divides the path from a car park, and reach the Grandstand on Glencruthery Road. The Tourist Trophy was founded in 1907 (the Gordon Bennett Cup Eliminating Trials had been held before then) and uses public roads for its race.

Pass the Grandstand and police station, and continue to walk along Glencruthery Road for about half a mile. You will be walking in the opposite direction to the TT course route.

At the first roundabout, before Governor's Hill, turn right into Victoria Road. A few yards downhill on the left you will see the entrance to Summerhill Glen, a green iron gate with blue seats either side. Go through the gate, and follow the Glen down to the bottom. It is one of 17 national glens across the island.

To exit the glen, walk down some steps and through the gate. Turn right into Summer Hill Road and then join the Queen's Promenade. Notice the Tramway stables, used by

Ann Reeder

the carthorses that pull the tram along the sea front in the summer. Immediately behind you, you will see the terminus for the Manx Electric Railway and the Horse Trams.

If you feel that you have walked far enough, in the summer season you may catch a horse tram to the tram stop opposite the Gaiety Theatre and resume this walk there, as described below.

If you continue on foot, cross over the Promenade to join the wide footpath alongside the cycle path, walking beside the bay for about one mile, and continuing into Central Promenade. Before leaving the Prom you will notice the distinctive Villa Marina across the road—a successfully refurbished conference and entertainment venue with attractive sheltered gardens. Then, after a low-rise row of shops and food outlets, you will enjoy the outstanding façade of the Victorian Gaiety Theatre, designed by Frank Matcham and opened in 1900 (see www.villagaiety.com).

Horse tram travellers will rejoin the walk here, at an alighting point. After you reach the War Memorial with its soldier high aloft, turn your back to the sea and cross over the roads and traffic island at the mini roundabout into Church Road. Pass the church, and reach the bend at the junction with Finch Road and Crellins Hill.

You have a choice of entrances to the Manx Museum now. If you are happy to climb the steep hill, turn to the right up Crellins Hill. Or for easier access, continue along Finch Road to enter the Chester Street car park and take the lift to the eighth floor, the walkway over the road and then the steps or ramp to the Museum.

Heritage Pub Walks in the Isle of Man

At the museum, make sure you first watch the evocative and informative film introducing the story of Mann, before exploring the social history galleries, the art gallery and the other exhibits.

After enjoying your visit to the Manx Museum, turn left at the front door and exit through the gate at the corner, turning left into Windsor Road. Walk past a row of shops, and cross over at the traffic lights to reach the pavement outside the Rosemount pub, before turning right into Woodbourne Road. Pass the end of Woodbourne Square with its palm trees, and turn left into Alexander Drive to return to the 'Woody'.

Walk 2 Peel—the sunset city

The Creek Inn and the House of Manannan and Peel Castle

Address: The Creek Inn, Station Place, Peel IM5 1AT
Web: thecreekinn.co.uk
Tel: 01624 842216
Hours: Every day from 10 am
Real ale: Okells and up to five guest beers; a Cask Marque pub

Food: Home-cooked pub food daily from noon to 10 pm
Parking: On-street parking or the public car park five minutes walk away at the Market Place

Situated on the Quayside, with views of Peel Hill and the Marina, the Creek Inn is open from 10 am every day. With locally brewed Okells ales and up to five ever-changing guest beers available all year round, the Creek Inn is a Real Ale drinkers' paradise, a Cask Marque pub and an active CAMRA supporter. Excellent home-cooked pub food is served every day from 12 noon until 10 pm from this family-run establishment, which has a traditional lounge. Local and UK bands play every weekend throughout the year and nightly during the TT and Manx Grand Prix, in the separate bar area. With a large outside seating area, the Creek Inn is the focal point of Peel down on the quay, especially during the TT and MGP. There are three darts teams and two pool teams. Car parking is available outside and along the quay.

Manx Heritage

House of Manannan

Address: Mill Road, Peel
Hours: Daily from 10 am to 5 pm all year, expect Christmas Day, Boxing Day and New Year's Day
Charge: Admission charged
Catering: Not available
Shop: Manx Heritage shop selling guide books, postcards, gifts, jewellery
Parking: At the site on Mill Road

Ann Reeder

The old railway station is the site of the award-winning House of Manannan. It evokes and clearly sign-posts so much of the island's enchanting history and particularly the story of Peel. Story tellers from the past, interactive displays, powerful videos and engaging props and technology introduce you to the Isle of Man's maritime history, Peel Castle and the city. You need two hours to cover this. The sea god, Manannan, after whom the museum is named, will welcome you to his Kingdom of Mann and with other characters from Manx history will guide you through 2,000 years of unique and fascinating heritage. A kipper factory. A Viking ship. A Steam Packet ship. The Chronicles of Mann. And much more.

Peel Castle

Address:	St Patrick's Isle, West Quay, Peel
Hours:	Daily from 10 am to 5 pm between Easter and October
Charge:	Admission charged
Catering:	Not available
Shop:	Limited kiosk selling guide books, postcards and souvenirs. Audio guides for hire
Parking:	At Fenella beach or on the breakwater

Located on St Patrick's Isle, which is now linked by causeway to Peel, the atmospheric site reveals places of worship and fortifications that have changed over centuries and now stand as silent witnesses to a chequered past. Inhabited since Celtic times and visited by St Patrick's followers, it has been fought over by Vikings, Norse, Scots, English, Irish and French. The subject of many excavations, you can follow an audio-guide around the 'island', so that this significant site, one of Mann's main heritage sites, can be unravelled for you. There was a

Celtic Christian community, now manifest in the ruins of St Patrick's Church, the Round Tower and St Patrick's Chapel; and you can see evidence of Norse fortifications, the beautiful shell of St German's Cathedral dating in part from the twelfth century and now a regular backdrop for summer open-air performances of Shakespeare's plays, medieval fortifications evident in the Gatehouse and Curtain Wall, and artillery fortifications of the sixteenth century and later. You need an hour to enjoy fully the wonderful setting and the amazing ruins.

The walk (Medium; 4 miles; full day)

Peel is a fascinating city to explore. It has quaint narrow streets; a marina, quay and jetty; the historic castle; a sandy and a shell-strewn beach; and beautiful sunsets. The first stop after your visit to the Creek Inn should be the House of Manannan so that you can understand some of the history of Peel and particularly Peel Castle before you visit the site on this walk. It is a varied walk around Peel Castle, up Peel Hill and Corrin's Hill, along the coast and inland along the river, offering attractive views around the west of the island. It is relatively demanding as it has a few climbs and you need to take care while walking round St Patrick's Isle and Peel Castle.

WALK 2

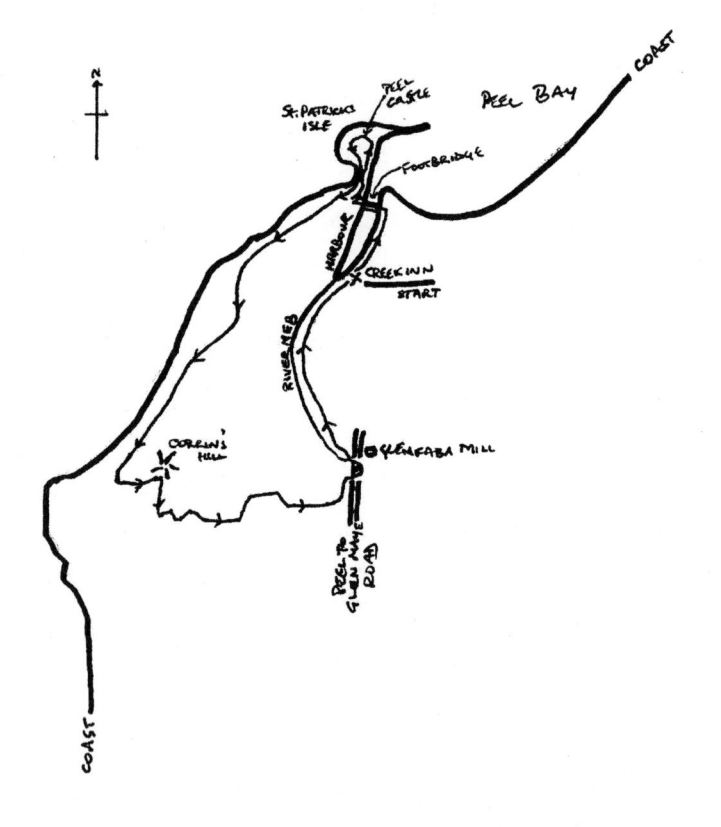

Heritage Pub Walks in the Isle of Man

Cross the road from the Creek Inn to visit the House of Manannan, noticing the plaque on the old station buildings to mark the centenary of the Peel Railway Station Building (1908-2008). After an exploration of this part of the Story of Mann and with a greater understanding of the intriguing ruins of Peel Castle that lie ahead, continue ahead into East Quay. Replica Viking ships may be anchored here. Follow the road with the Marina on your left, passing the Leece Museum, a Sailors' Shelter and a memorial to the 'seamen of this island lost at sea in war and peace', including those who saved the lives of more than 150 passengers of the RMS Lusitania on 7 May 1915.

At the bend in the road and with the sandy beach and prom ahead and to your right, cross over the footbridge to the left, at the entrance to the Marina. On West Quay, turn right in the direction of the castle, taking the causeway to St Patrick's Isle.

Take in a visit to Peel Castle, passing the sun dial near the entrance and listening out for the Mauthe Dhoog or Moddey Dhoo (the black dog), which is said to haunt this area, particularly the old Guard Room in the Gate House in the evening.

Collect an audio-guide at the ticket kiosk or the Peel Castle Trail leaflet in order fully to appreciate the rich history of this historic site. For example, the grave of the Pagan Lady was discovered in one of the digs here, a rich Viking woman who was buried in a wonderful necklace of glass and amber beads and with her cooking spit and other possessions. Allow an hour to explore the site and take in the marvellous views of the city, the west coast and the hills of the central valley.

Having enjoyed your visit to the Castle, continue along the causeway. On reaching the breakwater turn left to go through the gap in the wall and walk around the outside of Peel Castle, looking out for the Postern Gate, the tiny creek in the rocks which could be used as an emergency exit by boat; and for seals in the water and for wildflowers amongst the rocks and grass in the summer.

Having walked round nearly all the perimeter of the castle descend the steps onto Fenella beach looking out for attractive shells and cross the beach to a car park.

Take the footpath directly opposite and climb towards Peel Hill. Keep to the path on the right so that you can enjoy the coastal views and then make for Corrin's Folly on Corrin's Hill. Situated nearly 500 feet above sea level, it was built in 1806 by Thomas Corrin of Knockaloe, a small village to the south of Peel. The story goes that he was a Non-conformist who wanted to bury his family away from consecrated ground. His wife and daughters were buried there and he was later, having initially been buried in the churchyard. Whatever the truth behind Corrin's Folly, it is an outstanding landmark from sea and land, and the views from it are worth the climb. From the summit you can see over the quaint streets and roof tops of the city, the fishing boats which use Peel harbour, and the central valley, including the church of St John's and the flagpole of Tynwald Hill. You also cannot fail to miss the unfortunately tall power station chimney, about which there has been much controversy. Views to the north take in the coast up to Jurby Head, while on a clear day to the south you can see Milner's Tower on Bradda Head, and the peaks of Cronk-ny-Arrey-Lhaa and South Barrule.

From Corrin's Folly, take the grassy path along the coast going south. The complex among the trees is the Knockaloe

Heritage Pub Walks in the Isle of Man

Experimental Farm, run by the Department of Agriculture of the Manx Government, but used as an internment camp during the first world war. The path divides; avoid the temptation to continue along the coast! Turn left on a double track among the bracken and descend towards a cottage and the road, taking almost a back hand bend left, then at the corner of the stone wall, turn right. Enjoy the views of the coast, the city and the hills.

At the next junction take the right hand, lower path and just over the wooden stile in the wall, swing right to join the stony track to the cottage and the road. At the house, take the footpath to the left and look up at Corrin's Folly, where you have been. At the corner by two gateways turn right and continue down the track, which curves round to the right and narrows. Through the gate you can glimpse the beach, the city and the hills. The road turns left and has a gentle gradient downhill. Join the more made up track at a couple of gates and pass the gates to a restored landfill site. The track swings left and widens and you can see the River Neb below you.

At the white cottage join the main road and turn left. Cross over the road and the bridge and turn right down steps to the river at the Herring Way sign. Turn left under the road, after noticing the old Glenfaba mill with its dilapidated water wheel, and follow the disused track of the Douglas to Peel railway line back to the quay. The railway closed in 1972 and its route has become the Heritage Trail.

Further along the old line, a wooden fence diverts you away from the disused track onto the riverside path and over the river and culvert. Continue the gentle stroll along the bank of the river passing a row of cottages, a reservoir for the power

Ann Reeder

station and a light industrial estate. You will notice the kipper factories and shops of Devereau's and Moores near the entrance to the estate.

Where the river emerges into the quay, cross over Mill Road and keep on the right hand side of the Marina, walking towards Station Place and the Creek Inn.

Walk 3 Castletown—the ancient capital

The Sidings Inn and the Nautical Museum, Castle Rushen, the Old House of Keys and the Old Grammar School

Address: The Sidings Inn, Victoria Road, Castletown IM9 1EF
Tel: 01624 823282
Hours: Daily from 11.30 am to 11.30 pm
Real ale: Bushy's Bitter, Ruby Mild and Castletown Bitter plus up to six guests
Food: Served day-time and occasional evenings

Parking: Limited in the station approach; travel by steam train in season.
Car park on the route of the walk at the Parade, Market Place or Farrants Way, off Queen Street

The Sidings Inn is located on the approach to the Steam Railway station in Castletown. It has a beer garden. It shows live sport on TV, has occasional live music and a weekly quiz on Tuesday evenings. It is a free house and serves Manx and UK real ales.

Manx heritage

The Nautical Museum

Address: Douglas Street, Castletown
Hours: Daily from 10 am to 5 pm between Easter and October
Charge: Admission charged
Catering: Not available
Shop: Small shop
Parking: Limited on-street parking or car park at the Parade or the Market Place

This is much more than a boathouse. Built in 1789, it houses the eighteenth century armed yacht, the Peggy, which was owned by Captain George Quayle. He was an influential figure on the island and lived in the adjacent Bridge House, which has a surprising history to tell. The museum has exhibits in the intriguing Quayle and Cabin Rooms and the Sail-maker's Loft.

Heritage Pub Walks in the Isle of Man

Castle Rushen

Address:	Castle Street, Castletown
Hours:	Daily from 10 am to 5 pm between Easter and October
Charge:	Admission charge
Catering:	Not available
Shop:	Small shop selling guide books, postcards and souvenirs
Parking:	Car parking at Market Place or the Parade

Castle Rushen, built largely in the 13th and 14th centuries, is one of the most complete and best preserved medieval castles in the British Isles. Used as a home, a fort, a court and a prison, the Story of Mann uses tableaux to tell its tales, featuring the political and religious life of the island and showing the reign of kings, bishops and Lords of Mann. The castle played an important role in the English Civil War when home to the Stanleys. On a clear day, there are outstanding views from the inner gatehouse.

The Old House of Keys

Address:	Parliament Lane, Castletown
Hours:	Daily between Easter and October; regular 'sittings' during the day which are limited to 22 people
Charge:	Admission charge
Catering:	Not available
Shop:	Not available
Parking:	Car parks at the Market Place or the Parade

If you cannot vote often enough, this one is for you! You will be welcomed by the costumed Secretary of the House, before you join in the debates and cast your votes on a series

Ann Reeder

of significant pieces of legislation in the island's history. These include the Election Bill of 1880 that made the Isle of Man the first country in the world to give women the vote in national elections, the vote to introduce motor racing on public roads, and the Income Tax Bill of 1960 that led to the development of the finance sector. This building was the seat of the Manx Parliament (the House of Keys) from 1709 until 1869.

The Old Grammar School

Address:	The Parade, near the quay, Castletown
Hours:	Daily from 10 am to 5 pm between Easter and October
Charge:	Free
Catering:	Not available
Shop:	Selling guide books, postcards, gifts. The Old Grammar School also houses an exhibition and a tourist information centre
Parking:	Car park at the Parade

This, one of the oldest roofed structures in the island, was built in the thirteenth century as St Mary's Chapel and was the town church from 1554 to 1698. Rows of benches and desks with ink wells reflect its later life as a Grammar School from 1702 until 1930.

The walk (Easy; 4.5 miles, plus optional extra 3 miles; full day)

This is a gentle but very interesting walk through the historic former capital of the island and along the coast. The route offers delightful coastal and mountain views. It is a walk you may enjoy at your leisure, taking in four of the Story of Mann sites on your way.

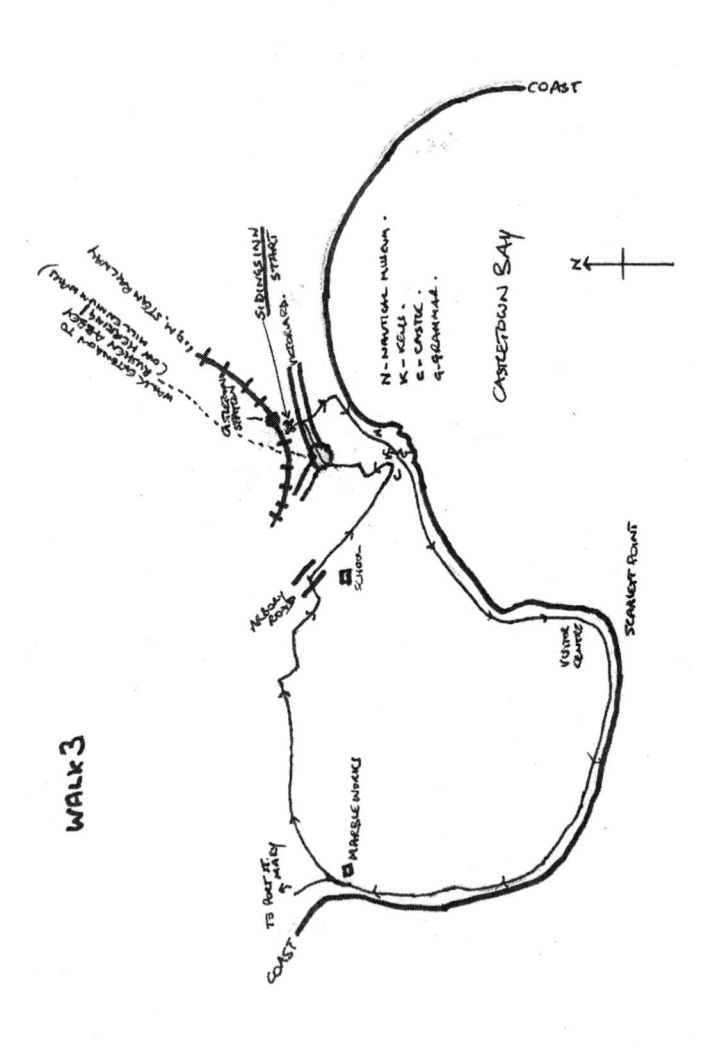

Heritage Pub Walks in the Isle of Man

Turn right out of the pub and cross over the main road, Victoria Road, to the road sign-posted Castletown Health Centre. Enter the footpath at the metal cycle barriers just beyond the health centre and next to the Coastguard Rescue Station. Emerge through two other metal cycle barriers onto Bowling Green Road, opposite Reef House and turn right.

Continue into Douglas Street, using the footpath on your right, following the curve of Castletown Bay and enjoying views across to Langness and the jetty of the harbour. The road bends right and becomes Bridge Street, and you will walk past the Nautical Museum. If you have time, do visit this remarkable part of the Story of Mann, home to nautical surprises.

Turn left at the end of this row, at Bridge Cottage, and cross the Silverburn River by the footbridge.

Once you have crossed the bridge, notice the police station, which is across the road to the right. It was built in 1901 to the design of Mackay Hugh Baillie Scott, the Victorian architect who trained and practiced on the island and was a contemporary of Archibald Knox. It complements the castle, in whose shadow it stands.

You now can choose whether and when to visit two adjacent sites of the Story of Mann—Castle Rushen and the Old House of Keys. Access to the Old House of Keys is timed because visitors are seated in the chamber to listen to stories from the parliament and to take part in votes, so you need to check the time of the next sitting. You might need to go straight into the Old House of Keys or you might want to visit Castle Rushen now and go back to the Old House of Keys for the next sitting or return to both or either of them when you come back to the

Ann Reeder

Square later on in the walk. Allow an hour for the castle and 45 minutes for the Old House of Keys.

After your visit(s) or if you decide to carry on with the walk immediately, face the Old House of Keys, walk round the right hand side of it and go through the gap to the Parade, a grass platform and car park above the harbour and jetty.

Facing out to sea, to the right you will see Scarlett Point with the disused lime kilns below it where your walk will take you. Langness juts out to sea ahead with the lighthouse that is such a feature of views from the hills in the south. You also can see the Herring Tower that was used to guide fishing boats into Derbyhaven on the sheltered side of the peninsular.

Ahead of you on the Parade is the Old Grammar School, part of the Story of Mann, but also a useful tourist information centre. Stay a while to explore this little gem before heading along the coast.

With your back to the sea, make for the gap in the buildings at the left hand corner of the square and follow the road into the corner of Market Square. Enjoy a view of the castle with the Elizabethan clock (noticing only one hand on its face) on the South Tower. You also will spot an empty plinth in the centre of the road; known as the candlestick, it was built in memory of Governor Cornelius Smelt in 1838, but apparently public subscription did not raise enough for his statue. There was an old Market Cross here, which was the site of a 'witch' burning in 1617.

Having explored the Square and with your back to the Castle, continue along Queen Street, following the signpost to the Scarlett nature trail, shown as being one mile away. This is part

Heritage Pub Walks in the Isle of Man

of the Isle of Man Coastal Path. The road goes behind coastal cottages in between which views open up of rocky pools on the shoreline and, out to sea, Langness and Castletown Bay. If you look behind you, the independent school, King William's College, and Castletown are visible.

As you reach Scarlett Point, you can see the remains of old lime kilns. You may follow the nature trail here. The visitors centre is open from late May until late September daily, except Monday, from 2 pm until 5 pm. There are geological displays, a trail, a shop and a warden in attendance. Limestone rock pavements are visible and you can see shags, cormorants, various gulls, oyster catchers, ringed plover and various ducks.

From Scarlett nature reserve, continue along the coast, passing the pink tower ruins of a coastguard station. A gap in the wall gives wonderful views of Chicken Rock lighthouse (six and a half miles away), the Calf of Man, Port St Mary, Fleshwick Bay, the Howe and Bradda Head to the south, as well as Langness behind you—a delightful sweep of the coast.

Continue along the grassy path (which is actually a part of the nature trail) along the shore on the left-hand or seaward side of the wall. There are several ruined buildings here, the remains of a wartime radio station. On a clear day you can see South Barrule to the left, and to the north Snaefell (the peak with the two radio masts) and other northern hills, as well as the 'Witches Mill' in Castletown, near which you will walk.

Continue along the coastal path and climb the stile over the stone wall. Skirt the arable field on the seaward side and climb another stone stile at the end of the field. Earthworks in the area such as a fort and ditch may date from Viking times. Drop

Ann Reeder

down towards the sea to cross the next wall by a stile, below the Strictly Private sign, at the boundary of the Poyllvaaish Quarry of the Manx Marble and Granite Co Ltd, and continue along the shore. Poyllvaaish translates as Death Pool or Bay of Death, reflecting stories of shipwrecks and pirates or the black marble of the sea bed. The quarry provided marble for the steps at St Paul's Cathedral in London, a gift from Bishop Wilson.

Take the footpath to the right, signed Castletown, and cross the fields towards the 'Witches Mill', crossing the stile and following a well-defined track besides a steam. Built in 1828 as a flour mill, the windmill fell into disuse later that century and was a witches' museum for a few years in the mid twentieth century.

Emerging on Arbory Road, turn right, passing Castle Rushen High School and the swimming pool. The main road bends to the right to Farrants Way, but you continue straight ahead into Arbory Street, the pedestrianised shopping street that continues into Market Square.

On emerging into the Square, you will see a plaque to commemorate John Wesley, founder of Methodism, who visited the Isle of Man in the 1770s and preached in front of the castle wall.

Unless you need to visit the castle and/or Old House of Keys, turn left into the castle gardens, using a path through the filled in moat; warning: the path closes at 4 pm. The footpath emerges from the castle grounds onto the road by the harbour. Turn left to pass the Legion gardens in the shelter of the castle wall.

If you are visiting the sites next, walk round the castle to the entrance of Castle Rushen and/or the Old House of Keys.

Heritage Pub Walks in the Isle of Man

Continue after the visits round the outside of the castle, inland along the quayside, passing the gate where the footpath through the castle gardens emerges and the Legion gardens.

At the end of the road, turn right to cross the road bridge over the Silverburn River.

Turn left onto Victoria Road, keeping the river on your left, and note the homes opposite, built out of the old Castletown Brewery that existed on this site from the 1760s to 1986.

[If you have time and want to take in Rushen Abbey, another of the Story of Mann sites, continue straight ahead at the bridge beside the roundabout. You will join the lower stretch of the Bayr ny Skeddan (the Herring Way from Peel to Castletown). This follows the Silverburn River, a footpath over a field and a track for a mile and a half to reach Rushen Abbey. This is another of the island's most important religious sites, the ruins of a medieval abbey. There are illuminating panels and fascinating interactive displays for all ages to help you find out about life in the Abbey and what the buildings were like. You may be surprised to discover the uses to which the buildings around the site had been put in the last two centuries. The heritage site also includes detailed information panels about the archaeological excavations and is set in attractive gardens. Then carry on along the river to marvel at the late fourteenth century Monks Bridge, before returning downstream to Castletown.]

Back at the roundabout, turn left if you have taken the detour to Rushen Abbey. If not, turn right, remaining on Victoria Road. Before you reach the petrol garage, turn left towards the railway station and back to the Sidings.

Walk 4 Tynwald—Parliamentary ceremonial

The White House Hotel and Tynwald Hill at St Johns, along the Heritage Trail

Address: The White House Hotel, Tynwald Road, Peel IM5 1LA

Awards: Isle of Man CAMRA Pub of the Year 2010 for the third year running

Tel: 01624 842252
Hours: Daily from 11 am until midnight
Real ale: Okells Bitter, Bushy's Bitter and Mild, and five guests such as Moorhouse's Pride of Pendle and Timothy Taylor's Landlord
Food: Not available
Parking: On-street parking or public car park at the Market Place

This is a Real Ale drinker's paradise, an unpretentious pub with the emphasis on a wide range of beer. Okells and Bushy's beers are served, as well as a large number of guest beers that change regularly and are written up on a large chalk board. The long-serving landlord has had more than one thousand guest beers on tap during his time at the pub. The White House has an old style multi-roomed central servery. The delightful snug, the Captain's Cabin, has its own bar and is entered from the street rather than through the main entrance. There is darts, pool, a TV for sport and music most Saturday nights.

Manx heritage

Tynwald Hill, St Johns

Address: Peel Road, St Johns
Hours: Daily all year
Charge: Free
Catering: Not available
Shop: Not available
Parking: Car park outside the arboretum, behind the church

Ann Reeder

Set in the Central Valley, closer to Peel than to Douglas, the village of St John's plays host to the annual Tynwald Day, on the Monday closest to the Manx National Day—5 July, (but previously on Old Midsummer Day—24 June). Tynwald, like the Icelandic Althing, an open air gathering, is derived from the old Norse Thing-vollr, a Law Hill. Tynwald now refers to the Assembly as well as the place of the gathering. Once a year the Lord of Mann (the Queen, the UK Head of State) or her representative, the Governor, the two Deemsters, the Coroners, and Members of the House of Keys and of the Legislative Council gather to promulgate the Acts passed by the Manx Parliament during the preceding year. The title of each Act is read in both Manx and English.

A service is held in St John's Church, where you will find named seats for the dignatories, and there is a fair on this public holiday. An exhibition on the history of Tynwald and of Tynwald Day stands in the church. Close by is the arboretum, established to commemorate the Millennium of the Tynwald in 1979. It contains trees sourced from the seventeen parishes and across the world, and plaques indicate the type of tree, its origin and which visiting dignitaries planted it.

Heritage Trail

The Heritage Trail was opened in the Year of Railways in 1993. The Isle of Man Railway Company Limited was formed in 1870, reached Peel in 1873, Port Erin in 1874, Ramsey in 1879 and Foxdale (via St John's) in 1886. It was closed in 1972 and the track was removed, apart from the Douglas to Port Erin line which still runs. Public rights of way were introduced over the disused sections.

The walk (Medium; 7 miles; half day)

The walk follows the old railway line from Peel through the centre of the island and turns into the open space at St John's before following the main road back into Peel where views open up to Peel Hill and the hills of the central valley. Although the Heritage Trail starts at Braddan Bridge, west of Douglas and goes just under 10 miles through the Central Valley to Peel, on this walk you will follow it only between Peel and St John's. This is a level walk that is clearly way-marked, initially along the River Neb, but it is a longer walk than the majority in this book and includes some pavement walking along a main road.

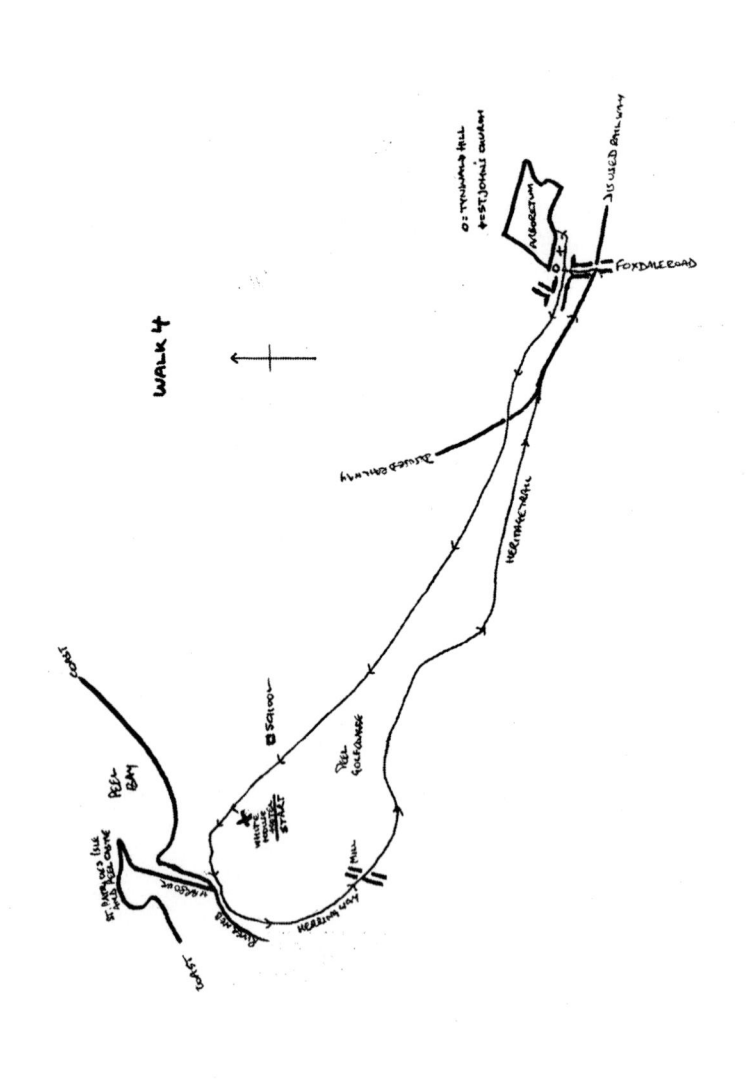

Turn left outside the White House and follow the road downhill, Douglas Street. With the Peel Castle Hotel on your right, turn left to skirt St Peter's Church wall, keeping the church on your right. Turn right into Lake Lane to reach the road on the landside of the House of Manannan, Mill Road, beside the old station buildings.

Continue ahead through the traffic lights, and pass Devereaus then Moores kipper factories. Do not cross the bridge at the head of the marina, near the old large anchor, but turn left at the signpost by the kipper factory fence, marked 'public footpath to Glenfaba'. Walk into an industrial estate with the power station chimney ahead of you and the river Neb on your right. Do not be deceived by the unattractive entrance to the trail, as you will soon enter the trail proper.

Continue along the river bank to a fenced weir and a blue lamp column, reaching a wooden finger post marked with the outline of a steam engine to denote the Heritage Trail. The trail follows the route of the old railway line between Douglas and Peel. The post also is marked with the sign of the Bayr ny Skeddan (the Herring Way from Peel to Castletown), which you will have taken for the first few yards.

Drop down along the river bank to follow the steam heritage railway trail, now without its rails. Pass the ruins of the mill and continue forward, ignoring signs to the right that would take you on the coastal footpath around Peel Hill and to Glen Maye on the Herring Way.

Continue ahead until you emerge from the track through a five bar gate below Slieu Whallian (the conifer plantation covered hill above St John's) into a gravel car park. Walk onto

Ann Reeder

the tarmac road, which curves round to the left and reach the Foxdale Road near a Forestry Commission site.

Turn left along the pavement towards the settlement of St John's, on the main road through the Central Valley, at the site of the Tynwald ceremony.

Spend some time here exploring the arboretum that was planted to commemorate the millennium of Tynwald in 1979. Visit the church of St John's, noting the seats that are allocated to each Member of the House of Keys (the lower house of parliament), the Senators (members of the upper house) and the Deemsters (judges); the arms of the Lords of Mann and the Lieutenant Governors; and the windows depicting Christian saints after whom the parishes are named. Finally follow the processional way to visit Tynwald Hill, a tiered mound on which the annual ceremony is held.

Having explored St Johns and with the church behind you, walk back to Peel along the main road, benefiting from pavements all the way. You will notice Corrin's Folly ahead of you.

When you reach a quarry on your right, you could take a footpath to the left to rejoin the Heritage Trail back to Peel. Alternatively you can continue on the shorter route along the road. If you keep on the road, after two and a half miles or so, you will pass the cemetery on the outskirts of Peel then the Queen Elizabeth II High School. Continue ahead into the town, down Tynwald Road, until you reach the White House on your left.

Walk 5 Laxey—the Lady Isabella

The Shore Hotel and the Laxey Wheel and Mines

Address: The Shore Hotel, Old Laxey IM4 7DA
Tel: 01624 861509
Hours: Monday to Sunday from noon to midnight
Real ale: Laxey Brewery's Bosun
Food: Pub style food is served from noon until 2.30 pm daily; Tuesday evening is 'Curry Night' from 6 pm to 8.30 pm
Parking: At the pub

Ann Reeder

This is a small village pub down in the harbour area. It has a microbrewery and sells its own Bosun Bitter. Its one room is lined with nautical memorabilia including maps. A river runs alongside, and there are wooden tables on a grassy area on its bank. There is occasional live music, piped music, a darts board and a winter darts league. The pub also has an extensive selection of whisky.

Manx heritage

The Great Laxey Wheel and mines trail

Address:	Mines Road, Laxey
Hours:	Daily from 10 am to 5 pm from Easter to October
Charge:	Admission charged
Catering:	Not available
Shop:	Limited at ticket kiosk
Parking:	Limited parking near the Wheel off Mines Road or at Dumbell's Row at the beginning of Mines Road

Across the island you can find evidence of Mann's long history of mining of lead, zinc and silver. The largest and most awesome attraction is the Great Laxey Wheel, otherwise known as the Lady Isabella, after the wife of the Governor in 1854 when the wheel opened. It is the largest surviving waterwheel in Europe, and was used to pump water from the Laxey mines. Up the valley from the wheel, you can enter a mine adit (entrance) for a short distance and downstream from the wheel you can see the remains of the old washing floors and a smaller water wheel.

The walk (Medium; 3.5 miles; half day)

This is a shorter walk but it does involve gradients. It follows the glen down to the sea, the harbour and the Prom before heading back up hill, affording glimpses of the Laxey Wheel. The walk takes in a visit to the Laxey Wheel, an adit at the mines and the washing floors.

WALK 5

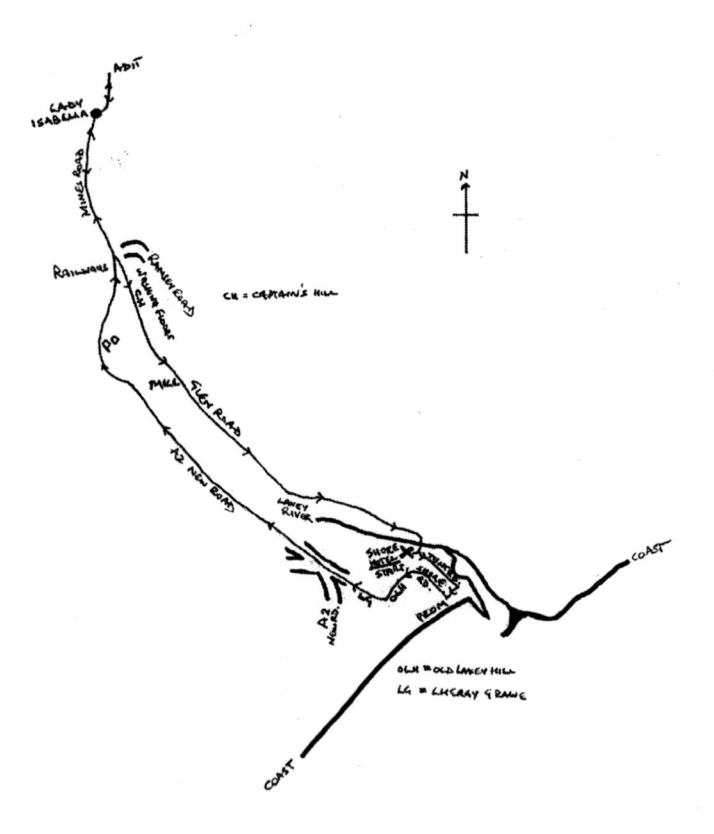

CH = CAPTAIN'S HILL

OLH = OLD LAXEY HILL
LG = LUCRAY GRANE

Heritage Pub Walks in the Isle of Man

Leave the pub by the front door and cross the road into Tent Road, with the river on your left, making for the harbour and the beach. Once at the sea, take in a short stretch of the Prom and turn right into Shore Road.

At the end of Shore Road, turn left up hill, Old Laxey Hill, taking care because there are no pavements. Turn right to walk up Lhergy Grawe. This lane was unnamed until as recently as 2008 when the Commissioners consulted residents and others to find some history about the area in order to select a name.

At the top of Lhergy Grawe, turn right into New Road, using the footpath on the right to walk to Laxey for about one and a half miles. Turn right over the bridge and cross the electric railway (listen for the whistle before crossing).

Turn left in to the Mines Road, walking past Dumbell's Row. This became known as Ham and Egg Terrace because of the number of women (many of them miners' wives) who opened their homes to provide refreshments to the tourists who descended upon the wheel in Victorian times.

Soon after passing the Laxey and Lonan Heritage Trust's information centre and shop, fork right down a footpath marked Laxey Wheel and follow to the entrance to climb to the top of this incredible feat of engineering and design. Go further up the valley to enter the mine adit, wearing the bright yellow hard hat that will be provided.

After visiting this part of the Story of Mann, retrace your steps to the end of Mines Road. Cross the rail and road ways, and walk to the left hand side of the shops into Captain's Row on

Ann Reeder

Captain's Hill. Almost immediately, walk through a gate to visit the Washing Floors and the Lady Evelyn or the Snaefell wheel, a smaller water wheel than the Lady Isabella. Cross the wooden bridge and come back onto Captain's Hill up a pathway then through a gap in a stone wall.

Turn left downhill for about one mile to the end of Captain's Hill, taking care over the lack of a pavement. At the crossroads, turn left into Glen Road, cross the bridge and turn right at the Laxey Woollen Mills. Founded by John Ruskin in 1851, they still produce Manx tartan today on original looms. Continue along Glen Road, eventually benefitting from a pavement, through a collection of houses.

When you reach Laxey Association Football Club and community grounds on the left, enter the playing fields if you want to avoid a section of the roadway, and follow Glen Road down, keeping the wall on your right.

Emerge from the playing field and continue along Glen Road to reach a bridge by the Mona Lisa restaurant and turn right onto Old Laxey Hill to return to the Shore Hotel.

Walk 6 Ramsey—'down the north'
The Trafalgar Hotel and the Grove Museum

Address: The Trafalgar Hotel, West Quay, Ramsey IM8 1DW
Tel: 01624 814601

Hours:	Mondays to Thursdays from 11 am to 11 pm, Fridays from 11 am to midnight, Saturdays from 11 am to 12.15 am and Sundays from 11.30 am to 11 pm
Real ale:	Okells Bitter, Moorhouse's Black Cat Mild and two guests
Food:	Not available
Parking:	At the Market Place

The Trafalgar is one of the oldest pubs in the town, and stands alongside the inner harbour. It is a traditional, small and friendly free house and is a great pub for real ale drinkers. It has regularly been awarded the Cask Marque.

Manx Heritage

The Grove, a museum of Victorian lifestyles and rural life and gardens

Address:	Andreas Road, Ramsey
Hours:	Daily from 10 am to 5 pm from Easter to October
Charge:	Admission charge
Catering:	Conservatory Restaurant
Shop:	Manx heritage shop
Parking:	At the site

The Grove is an early Victorian country house. It was the summer retreat then home of a wealthy Victorian merchant, Duncan Gibb, and his family. Gibb made his money in Liverpool through shipping. Authentic period rooms reflect the typical home of a successful businessman. Outbuildings display agricultural equipment that is typical of the era and there are attractive country gardens and pasture stocked with Manx Loghtan sheep.

The walk (Easy; 4 miles; half day)

This is an easy walk around the harbour, along the sandy shore, through a magnificent park, around the town and along the Queen's Promenade. There are wonderful views of the bay and delightful gardens around an impressive lake. The town is known as Royal Ramsey because of two royal visits—Queen Victoria and Prince Albert in 1847 (looking inland you may spot Albert Tower on a hillside from time to time, built to mark the spot reached by Prince Albert on an unscheduled stop at Ramsey) and King Edward VII and Queen Alexandra sixty years later.

WALK 6

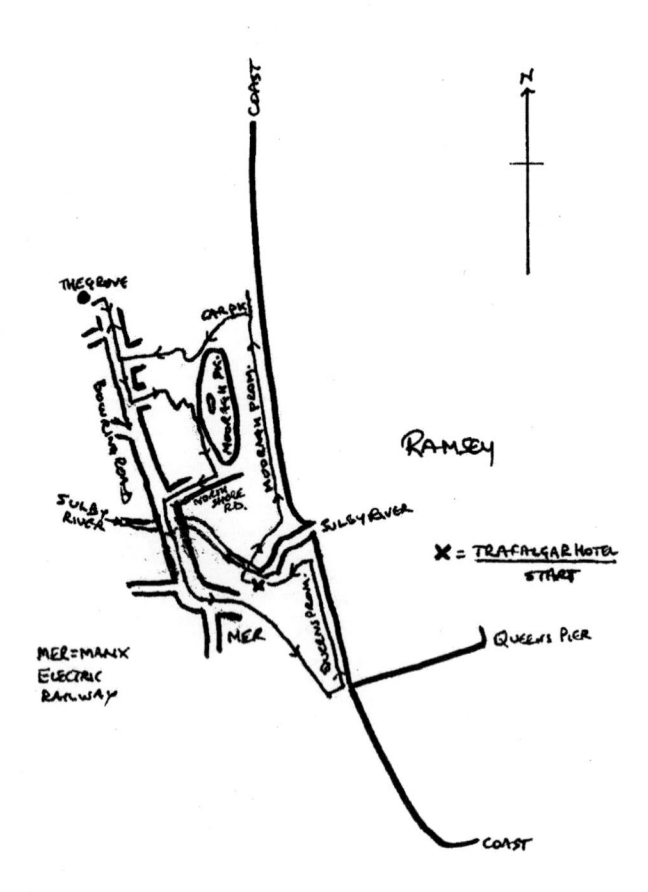

Heritage Pub Walks in the Isle of Man

Turn left outside the Trafalgar and walk along East Quay to the iron swing bridge. It was opened in 1892 and stretches 225 feet across the Sulby River between the inner and outer harbour. Cross over this bridge to reach the grassy area and continue to the Mooragh Promenade.

Follow the shoreline and enjoy a view of a stretch of the ten mile sweep of bay that extends to the Point of Ayre, a sandy shore 'down the north' at the edge of the northern plain.

Turn left at a T junction on the Prom to cross a car park and enter Mooragh Park at the further end. The park was created in the 1880s from reclaimed wasteland and includes 40 acres of attractive gardens and amenities such as a children's play area and paddling pool, miniature golf, a bowling green, tennis courts and a boating lake. You will return to the park later on this walk. At this stage you will pass through only for a short distance.

Continue straight ahead (do not take the left fork as this would take you along the seaward side of the lake) and aim for the tennis courts. As you reach the courts, turn right to take a footpath and steps up hill through trees and shrubs and exit the park through a yellow gate at the top into Grove Mount.

Turn left along Grove Mount to reach the main road, Bowring Road. Turn right at the junction, and walk a short distance (Bowring Road becomes Andreas Road) before crossing over to visit the Grove.

Having visited the Grove, turn right onto the footpath along the main road to walk back towards Ramsey town centre

Ann Reeder

(Andreas then Bowring Roads). After just over half a mile, you will pass Ramsey and District Cottage Hospital. Take a left turn into Cumberland Road and turn right into Bay View. Cross the grassy area and go through a gate to take the path down the hillside to enter Mooragh Park with the lake ahead of you.

Turn right at the bottom to walk through the park until you reach North Shore Road where you turn right, away from the sea. Rejoin the main road, Bowring Road, by the post office, and cross over the bridge over the Sulby River, this time at the end of the harbour, into Parliament Square. Walk along Queen's Pier Road for a short distance and continue through to Albert Square. Fork left into Albert Road and pass the terminus of the Manx Electric Railway, stopping off at the visitor centre at the station, where photos tell the story of the MER.

Continue along Albert Street into Waterloo Road before turning left into Queens Drive East to reach the Queen's Pier. Built in 1886 it stretched more than 2,000 feet into the sea to form a jetty for steamers in Victorian times. However its future has been in doubt for many years, and there has been a local campaign for its preservation and restoration.

Facing the pier, turn left to walk along Queen's Promenade, passing the swimming pool and St Paul's Church by the Market Place and follow the harbour-side back to West Quay and the Trafalgar.

Walk 7 Port St Mary—crofters' settlement

The Albert Hotel and Cregneash

Address: The Albert Hotel, Athol Street, Port St Mary IM9 5DS
Tel: 01624 832118

Ann Reeder

Hours: Monday to Thursday from 10.30 am to midnight, Friday and Saturday 10.30 am to 1 am and Sunday from noon to midnight
Real ale: Okells, Bushy's bitter and Old Bushy Tail, and typical guests: Old Speckled Hen, Bushy's guests and Okells guests
Food: Selection of homemade sandwiches available daily as well as scones freshly baked on the premises and cooked lunches from Monday to Saturday
Parking: On-street parking and car park at Athol Street

A traditional family run pub in the picturesque harbour village of Port St Mary. The landlord is proud of serving good quality ales in a clean, friendly environment. There are three well-appointed rooms and a bus stop just outside, so the Albert could be an ideal base; the family are keen walkers with an abundance of local knowledge. There are darts, pool, a juke box, a weekly quiz on Sundays at 8 pm, and Manx singing and language on the last Friday of the month. Parking is limited; on-street. There is a small beer garden and a covered smoking area.

Manx heritage

Cregneash Village Folk Museum

Address: Cregneash village, near Port St Mary
Hours: Daily from 10 am to 5 pm between Easter and September
Charge: Admission charged
Catering: Village Tea Rooms serving lunches and afternoon teas

Shop:	Cummal Beg ('Little Dwelling'), the information centre and museum entrance, sells Manx publications, gifts and souvenirs
Parking:	Five to ten minutes walk from the village on the main road

The Story of Mann comes to life in the manner of Cregneash, a typical nineteenth century crofting village with a 67 acre working farm, a flock of Loghtan sheep, roaming hens, weavers, a smithy, threshing machines and Harry Kelly's cottage. Harry Kelly was a Cregneash crofter and Manx speaker who died in 1935. His cottage contains furniture and equipment that mostly belonged to him and dramatically introduces you to a typical dwelling and lifestyle of that era.

Hosts greet you in dress typical of the Victorian villager. They would have been making a hard living in a tough environment. You can roam the site in the open air, witnessing the range of livelihoods needed for survival and self-sufficiency on land and from the sea. Enjoy the wonderful vistas over the fields and towards the sea.

You can gain an appreciation of what life must have been like in the informative and inspiring audio-visual, oral histories and photographic displays at Cummal Beg.

The walk (More challenging; shorter walk 5 miles; longer walk 8 miles; full day)

Step back in time and take the steam railway from Douglas to Port St Mary. A short walk from the station brings you to the beautiful bay and busy harbour of Port St Mary. It is your gateway to a dramatic coastline of rocky cliffs and coves and on to the crofters' settlement of Cregneash with its charming open air museum. This is a longer and more challenging walk than others in this book but it is extremely rewarding, with outstanding views to enjoy all the way. It is a beautiful and dramatic walk that starts along the island's coastal path, the Raad ny Foillan ('Way of the Gull'). It then skirts or crosses the Chasms, incredible rock fissures where extreme care is needed. Turning inland you will visit the Cregneash open air museum depicting a typical late nineteenth century crofters' village living off the land and sea. Returning to the coast, fantastic vistas open up of the south of the island, the west and east coast and even the highest mountain, Snaefell, in the north of the island. The walk gently follows a raised coastal walkway around the bay and harbour of Port St Mary to return up a slipway to the Albert Hotel, a pub where you might hear the Manx language spoken. It is recommended that a day is taken for this walk because it is up and down hill and around the rugged coastline. A refreshment break is possible in the café at Cregneash. You will need stout walking shoes and your binoculars for the outstanding views and birdlife.

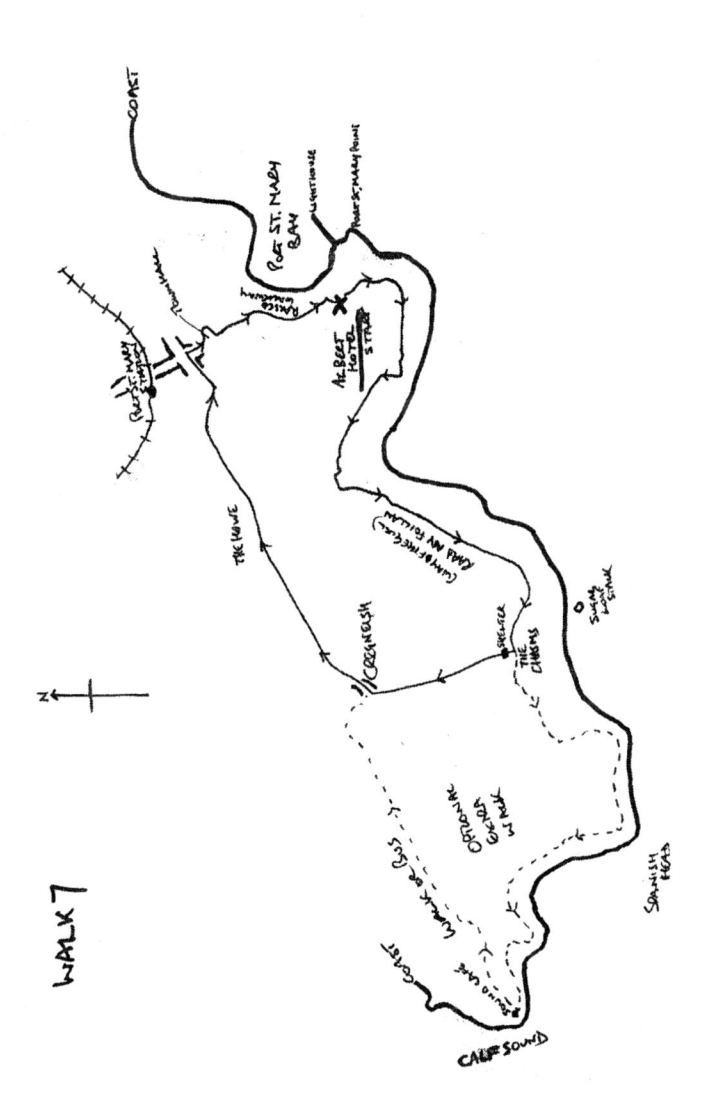

Ann Reeder

Turn right out of the Albert Hotel and walk along the street to Kallow Point, passing the RNLI shop at Port St Mary lifeboat station. There are good views to the east to Langness, and to the west. Pass the open space and follow the sign post for Port Erin 6.5 miles. Turn right along Clifton Road along the coast, which is part of the Raad ny Foillan ('Way of the Gull'). It becomes a track then a path between the golf course and the cliff, which you will follow closely.

Go through the kissing gate and turn left onto the pavement. Go through the Perwick Bay housing development bearing right, which is signed public right of way, and leave the development in the far right hand corner. Take this track between shrubs, go through the gate and turn left on the road downhill. Cross Glen Chass bridge and ignore the public footpath signs to left and right, and continue ahead.

You will reach a signpost for the Chasms at the turning point and the track narrows, becoming unsuitable for vehicles. Continue ahead on the coastal footpath, not the public footpath to the right. Go over the stile or through the gate into a series of meadows. After walking straight across several meadows the path becomes a walled lane. It then opens out into an open meadow, which you should cross diagonally to the left hand corner and continue along the cliff. There are spectacular coastal views. Stack Bay and Black Head are ahead of you. Turn right and go through a gate to ascend the cliff, but pause at the gate to have your first view of the Sugar Loaf stack. Many sea birds nest on the cliffs here. The final section of this path is rather a scramble; keep close to the wall, pausing to enjoy views of Port St Mary and the sweep of Perwick and Port St Mary bays. The path curves left, hugging the cliff top and the Sugar Loaf stack can be seen more clearly.

You may see boats carrying day trippers to or around the Calf of Man.

Warning—you are approaching the Chasms and if you enter them, you need to proceed with extreme care. Do not enter them if there is poor visibility. These are an area of subsidence and fissures in the rock with massive drops, but they can be skirted with care. The land around the Chasms has a wonderful covering of ling and gorse, purple and yellow intermingling in the summer-time. But don't be deceived by such beauty. The rocks on which they grow provide a very dangerous landscape. Take care crossing this area, and exit through a gate at the top of the area, near the shelter.

If you do not want to enter the Chasms, follow the path round the outside of the wall and head towards the building. It now provides a sheltered seat but used to be a café. Pause here to appreciate the dramatic landscape of the Chasms from the safety of the field—and to notice the warning given that persons visit only at their own risk and should proceed with caution.

Shorter walk

Turn inland towards Cregneash village and with your back to the sea at the disused café take the grass path diagonally to join the footpath uphill towards a stile and the radio beacon. You should have wonderful views to Scarlett, Langness and Castletown behind you. After you have crossed the stile, you will pass a corrugated building on the left and a car park and a white row of buildings to the right. Take in the views to the Calf of Man, and follow the road downhill to Cregneash, ignoring the public footpath sign to your left.

Ann Reeder

The first thatched and white-washed building you will pass on your left is Harry Kelly's Cottage, part of the open air part of the Story of Mann, featuring the lives and homes of upland crofters and fishing folk. Before visiting this cottage, go to the Story of Mann site entrance at Cummal Beg, the long pebble-dashed building at the fork in the road ahead, to buy tickets or show your pass or card. Spend a few minutes watching the informative and atmospheric film of the island's rural and fishing heritage before visiting the houses, workshops and farm. You need at least an hour for this stop.

Longer walk

To complete the longer and even more rewarding walk, pass the shelter at the Chasms and continue along the coast. Cross the wall at the end of the field by the steps and handrail. You will now be walking on Spanish Head, so-called because of the wreck of a Spanish galleon at this point around the time of the Armada.

Follow the path which hugs the coast, cross the stile or use the gate, enjoy a break on the bench then continue along the coast ignoring the gate to the right. There are more spectacular views of the cliff and the Sugar Loaf. The path descends, a stream is crossed and the path curves sharply left uphill. Keep ahead (not right) and fork left to continue along the coast to the top of Spanish Head, again pausing to enjoy the scenery. Further along the path the Calf of Man comes into view with Kitterland in the channel and the Sound café on the mainland.

The views are outstanding of the cliff, the coast and the island, the Calf of Man, and of the rocks offshore. Take care for the

Heritage Pub Walks in the Isle of Man

steep descent, benefiting from the holes cut in the side to keep a grip as you make for the Sound. At the foot of the hill there is a little bridge and a gate. Cross the stile, enjoy the stunning views, cross the next stile, keep to the coast and the further stile, skirt the boulder and arrive at the Sound after an outstanding walk from Port St Mary.

Seals often are to be seen relaxing on Kitterland. There are a number of memorials to tragedies in this treacherous channel between the Isle of Man and its Calf.

Rest a while at the Sound Café, have a comfort break, enjoy refreshments and explore the attractive hanging displays at the Sound before resuming your journey. If you have walked far enough, you may be able to take a bus up to Cregneash, the next part of the Story of Mann. Otherwise take the road for one mile uphill to Cregneash, the open air folk museum that covers rural life in the late nineteenth century.

You will need to buy a ticket or show your pass or card at Cummal Beg, the house that serves as the entrance to the Story of Mann site. Having watched the film and fully explored Cregneash village, whether you walked from the Chasms or the longer route via the Sound, your route back to Port St Mary will provide rewarding views and more easy-going walking on roads and paved footways.

Returning to the Albert Hotel from Cregneash from either the short or long walk, leave the village at the road beside St Peter's Church (noticing the green phone box!) and turn right to follow the road downhill towards Port St Mary. Pass the entrance to the visitors' car park and continue ahead, enjoying views of the northern hills, including Snaefell, and of Ganzey Bay.

Ann Reeder

You will begin to see Port St Mary to your right, and in the dip in the road, Milner's Tower on Bradda Head and the hotels and houses of Port Erin. Through the gap that is Fleshwick Bay, you can see the beautifully set Niarbyl on the west coast. The name Niarbyl means the tail, and refers to the rocky shoreline that juts out into the sea.

After walking through the hamlet of The Howe, you will benefit from a pavement for the next stretch of the walk. Take care on the narrow bend when the pavement has ended. Turn left at the bend into Plantation Road; do not turn right into Cronk Road. Continue downhill to the cross roads, and turn right at the stop sign next to the school (Scoill Purt Le Moirrey) into Station Road. After the pelican crossing, turn left into The Promenade.

Immediately after the Town Hall, take the footpath to the right downhill, keeping the low wall on your right. On joining the wide pavement, turn right behind the Town Hall, then take the steps at a lamp post to a slipway.

Go left down the slipway and turn right at the end of the slipway to join the raised walkway ('the Underway') around the inner harbour. Continue ahead along this section of the coastal path, the Raad ny Foillan ('Way of the Gull'), emerging up the slipway from Chapel Beach, opposite the Albert Hotel.

Walk 8 Port Erin—seaside elegance

The Bay Hotel and the Steam Railway Museum

Address: The Bay Hotel, Shore Road, Port Erin IM9 6HL
Awards: Joint runner up as Isle of Man CAMRA Pub of the Year 2010, regular CAMRA award winner and food award winner
Web: www.bushys.com
Tel: 01624 832084
Hours: Daily from noon to midnight but hours may vary

Ann Reeder

Real ale: Bushy's bitter, Bushy's Ruby Mild, Castletown bitter and Old Bushy Tail plus typical guests Bushy's Oyster Stout, Manx Pride and a permanent UK guest

Food: Traditional/gourmet Manx; summer daily noon to 2.30 pm and 6 pm to 8.30 pm; winter Friday, Saturday and Sunday from noon to 2.30 pm and Wednesday, Thursday, Friday, Saturday and Sunday from 6 pm to 8.30 pm

Parking: On-street parking and public car park on Station Road and Bridson Street

This is an imposing Victorian seaside pub, overlooking a popular and picturesque beach. One side is devoted to the service of real ales and ciders, the other is mainly a restaurant. An outside terrace offers wonderful views, as well as the chance for families to supervise kids playing on the beach. There are darts, a monthly pop quiz and live music monthly. A huge beach is but a stone's throw away. There is a partly covered smoking area.

Manx heritage

Port Erin Railway Museum

Address: Station Road, adjacent to the steam railway station
Hours: Daily from 10 am to 5 pm between April and November
Charge: Free
Catering: Station café
Shop: Gift shop
Parking: On Station Road

Located by the railway station in an old train shed, the museum explores the history of steam travel on the island and contains steam trains, original carriages, railway memorabilia, equipment and fittings, as well as an exhibition. It is adjacent to the maintenance yard, where you can see the active blacksmith's workshop looking after the working stock.

The walk (More challenging; 5 miles; half day)

This is a popular walk for understandable reasons. Port Erin is a beautiful seaside town with a stunning sandy beach and sheltered bay. There are outstanding coastal views and on a clear day you may enjoy views of the hills of Ireland and occasionally of Wales, as well as Mann. But like the walk from Port St Mary, this is not a walk for the faint-hearted! It includes steep stretches and jagged paths, part of the walk being along the Island's coastal path, the Raad ny Foillan ('Way of the Gull'). Don't forget your binoculars for this walk and wear strong shoes.

WALK 8

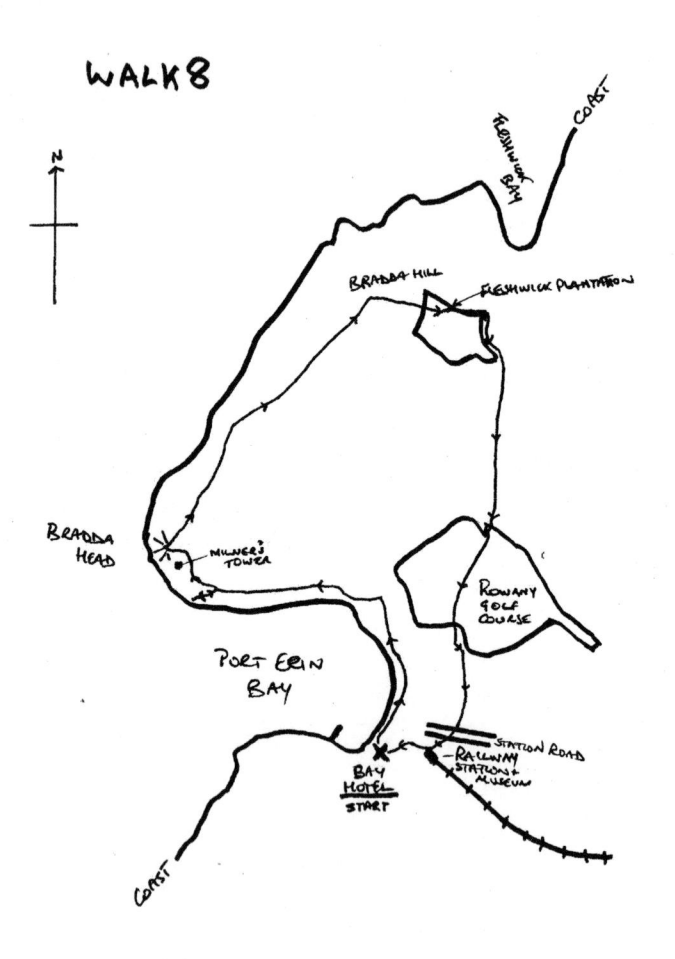

Heritage Pub Walks in the Isle of Man

Turn right out of the pub and walk across the beach or follow the promenade alongside the beach, aiming for the port (red) lighthouse at the head of the bay. Walk up the tarmac path or the steps to the right of the Cosy Nook Café to emerge at the flagpole. Turn left up the hill, passing the Port Erin Hotel on the right, go over the top of the hill then part of the way down and enter Bradda Glen on the left to join the footpath to Bradda Head and Milner's Tower.

On the opposite side of the bay you will see the quay used by the boats that take visitors to the Calf of Man, the island off the tip of the Isle of Man. You can spend a memorable day walking and relaxing on the Calf, a bird sanctuary. As you climb above the bay, you will begin to enjoy the delightful views of the Calf, a patchwork of purple, green and grey surrounded by rugged cliffs. The white tower indicates the Kitterland rocks in the straits between the Isle of Man and its Calf. There are strong currents, which have contributed to numerous tragic wrecks.

The well made up path climbs along the edge of the cliff. Around the corner Milner's Tower comes into view and a series of steps will help your ascent. At the junction take the right fork to Milner's Tower. Before that you can continue the short distance to the end of the lower path to enjoy the views of Port Erin, the Calf and a ruined copper mine, but you will then need to retrace your steps.

Continue on the cement path towards the wooden fence and the steps to meet the Coronation Path. Walk between the bracken and enjoy the view over Langness as well as Port Erin. The sea seems to be everywhere in sight.

Ann Reeder

Go through the chain fence in the stone wall, turn immediately right through the kissing gate, and then immediately walk left up a wide grassy gentle path. Go through two broken down walls and over a ridge and turn left at the footpath sign towards Milner's Tower on Bradda Head.

Marvel at the views from the Tower. The views are superb over the south of the island, to the Calf of Man and one of its lighthouses, up the coast to Niarbyl and Corrin's Tower near Peel, and along the east coast of Ireland. The tower is dedicated to 'William Milner in grateful acknowledgement of his charities to the poor of Port Erin and of his never tiring efforts for the benefit of Manx fishermen. Built by public subscription 1871'. Milner was a safe-maker from Liverpool, so the lock shape of the tower reflects his trade. He was a philanthropist and supported the town and cared for the welfare of sea-farers.

Leaving Milner's Tower, descend on the path north along the coast, heading for Bradda Hill. Make for the gate by the public footpath sign and turn left through the kissing gate and follow the line of the fence. Gorse and heather make a lovely summer carpet here.

Continuing along the right hand side of the fence, the path begins a gradual grassy climb on this sheep strewn hill. Take care, especially if children are with you, as you are not far from the cliff edge—fine if you are nimble footed sheep or sea birds but dangerously sheer for humans. The path gets rockier and less well-defined. Keep inland as you go over this rocky stretch and look out for the occasional outcrop of quartz among the slate and granite. The path becomes more clearly defined again.

Heritage Pub Walks in the Isle of Man

Ascend the path with the fence in view and enjoy the splendid views up the coast to the cottages at Niarbyl and Corrin's Folly, both worth a visit on another day; they are featured in this book.

Continue along the grassy path towards the hill and climb over the wooden gate at the corner of the field by the broken footpath sign. You are now on the cliff edge with the fence on the landward side of you and you begin a steep ascent of the second of three cliff tops on this stretch of the walk. Continue along the coastal path, downhill, taking particular care over the jagged rocks at the initial steep descent then continuing on a more gentle descent and the next climb. Port St Mary will come into view. At the corner of the field you will see a cairn ahead on Bradda Hill at 726 feet. Skirt this on the path which curves inland and becomes more gentle. The summits of Cronk-ny-Arrey-Lhaa and South Barrule are visible ahead.

Begin the descent, plunging through the heather and go through a broken down wall by a sign indicating a public right of way in both directions. It is a difficult descent because of heather and bracken. Aim for the buildings below, by the road, keeping Fleshwick Plantation to your right and with Fleshwick Bay to your left. The grassy slope may be slippery but try to enjoy the rewarding views of the south of the island. Go through the white wooden kissing gate and the meadow to the road.

Turn right along the road to the large stone house where you turn right at the public footpath sign and the sign declaring 'Unsuitable for motors'—always a good sign for walkers! Walk between the house and the outbuildings, then in front of the plantation. Pass a house with an old gas lamp and the track curves to the right where you join a road.

Ann Reeder

At the end of Ernie Broadbent Walk turn right. You are in Bradda East and the road climbs and narrows. Port Erin Bay and the Calf of Man come back into view. At Creg Cottage take the public footpath signed to the left and cross the field diagonally to your right. Go through a chain linked gate and reach the edge of the golf course.

Follow the golf course round to the right, to reach Rowany Drive. You will see a block of flats, Fairways Court on Rowany Drive, and at the bend in the road, turn to go down hill on Fairway Drive, noticing the view of the airport control tower and Langness.

On the next bend, turn left down a tarmac footpath, through metal barriers down hill along Harrison Street. At the bottom turn right and in twenty yards turn left into Bridson Street. At a T junction by the Haven pub, turn right to reach Port Erin station and the railway museum.

Having visited the railway museum, turn left onto Station Road and follow round to the left into Strand Road, towards the bay. At the T junction, with the beach ahead, turn left into Shore Road and continue back to the Bay Hotel.

Walk 9 Douglas—the age of the Victorians

The Rovers Return pub and Marine Drive and a ride on the steam railway

Address: The Rovers Return pub, 11 Church Street, Douglas IM1 2AG

Awards: Joint runner up as Isle of Man CAMRA Pub of the Year 2010

Ann Reeder

Tel: 01624 676459
Hours: Mondays to Thursdays from noon to 11 pm and Fridays to Sundays from noon to midnight
Real ale: Bushy's Bitter and Mild and up to three guests from the UK
Food: Served between noon and 2 pm from Mondays to Fridays
Parking: Public car park at Shaw's Brow

This is one of the oldest pubs in Douglas and is situated on a narrow cobbled lane close to the Town Hall. It is within a five to ten minutes walk of the railway station and quay. The Rovers Return is a traditional pub with a pleasant friendly atmosphere. A Bushy's tied house, it also has a range of regularly changing guest beers and seasonal beers. It gets very busy, with a mixed largely local customer base. There's a large lounge with Wi-Fi, a pool room and a couple of other bars. The pub was named, not after a pub on a popular TV soap, but after the football team supported by Bushy's founder, so there are Blackburn Rovers FC photos, paintings, shirts and mementos around the walls.

Manx Heritage

Marine Drive

Address: Douglas Head
Hours: Daylight hours
Charge: Free
Catering: Not available
Shop: Not available
Parking: On-street parking at Douglas Head

Heritage Pub Walks in the Isle of Man

In the late 1800s, the Victorian tourists enjoyed scenic drives and outings. The stretch of cliff top beyond the popular tourist spot of Douglas Head provided a wonderful viewpoint, and Douglas Head Marine Drive Ltd was formed in 1889 with a view to developing this stretch as a scenic route. An electric tramway with access by an inclined railway at each end was built from Douglas to Port Soderick, a pebble beached bay at the end of a pretty glen, only about three miles from the capital and popular resort. The tramway went into decline and was turned into a road in 1956, only to be closed in 1976 because of the danger of rock falls. Nevertheless it is a wonderful place for walking along the coast, and it now forms part of the Way of the Gull, the Raad ny Foillan ('Way of the Gull'), round the island's coastline.

The steam railway

Address:	Railway Terrace, at the junction of Peel Road, Athol Street, Lord Street and Bridge Road, Douglas, at the end of North Quay
Hours:	Daily from Easter to September; selected days in March, October and November, plus specials such as Santa Specials in December
Charge:	Fares charged. Island Rover tickets available; see www.iombusandrail.info
Catering:	Station café in Douglas
Shop:	Not available
Parking:	Limited parking at the railway station; public car park at Shaw's Brow

The line opened in 1874 and runs nearly sixteen miles between Douglas and Port Erin, making it the longest narrow gauge steam railway line in the British Isles. The journey from

Ann Reeder

Douglas to Port Erin takes approximately one hour. There are official stops at seven stations such as Port Soderick and Castletown and request stops at four specified halts. If you travel on a train pulled by No 4 'Loch', you are being carried by one of the original engines.

The walk (Medium; 5 miles; plus possible 3 miles back if the steam railway is not running; half day)

The penultimate walk in this book breaks the pattern. It may be circular or you may be able to return by steam train from Port Soderick to Douglas in the summer. The walk provides stunning views across Douglas and the northern hills, then southwards along the rocky coast from the coastal footpath before dropping to the shore and climbing through a glen to the railway. A return walk partly beside the railway would be possible but would require walking along the main road, the Old Castletown Road, for some distance.

WALK 9

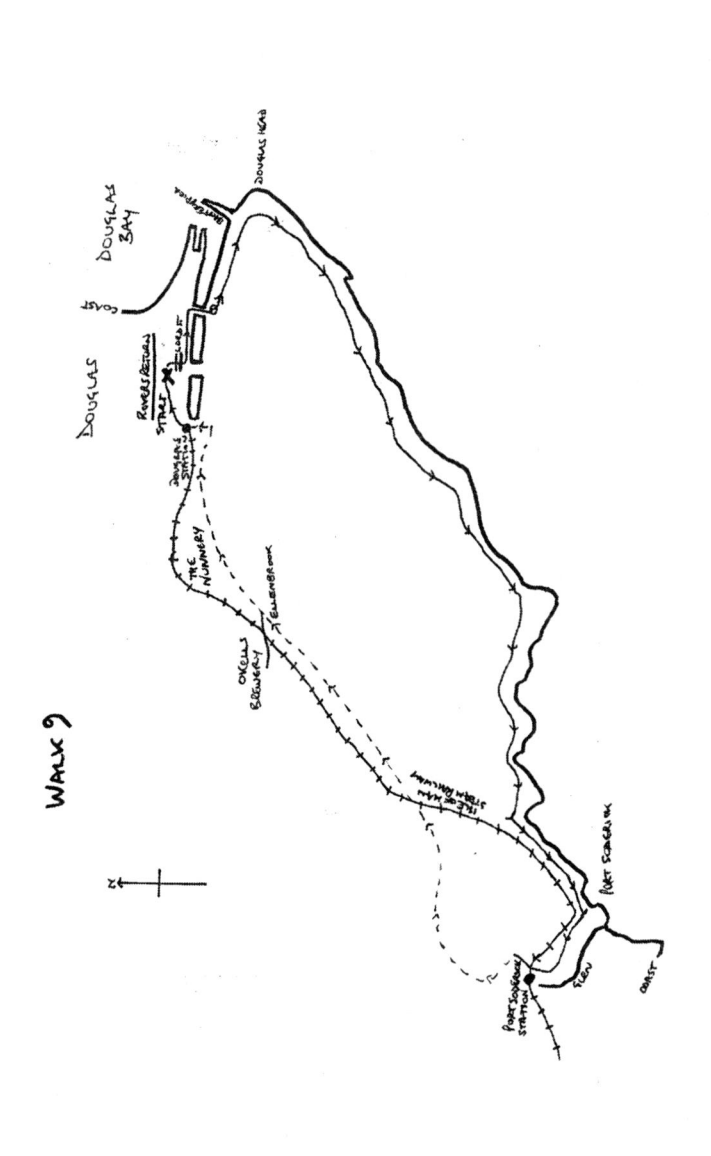

Ann Reeder

Turn right out of the Rovers Return and cross over Lord Street, noticing the statue of George Formby, before following Ridgeway Street down to the quay. At the T junction, observe that the railway station, the terminal of the Isle of Man Steam Railway, is at the end of Douglas Marina (the inner harbour), set back in the corner to the right. You will return by steam train later.

Turn left at North Quay, and cross over the lifting bridge (completed in 1999) at the seaward end of the Marina. Turn left at the mini roundabout and walk along South Quay towards the Battery Pier, passing a memorial to the Herring Fleet Disaster in 1787, in which, it is estimated, 161 people died when fishing boats were lost in a sudden storm. The memorial is nearly opposite the Lifeboat Station. The 'National Institution for the Preservation of Life from Shipwreck' was formed on the Isle of Man in 1824, a forerunner of the Royal National Lifeboat Institution. Sir William Hillary, one of the instigators of the service, lived in Douglas and carried out some of the rescues. The Tower of Refuge in Douglas Bay is a reminder of the dangers shipping has faced over the years and the important contribution which lighthouses, beacons and lifeboats have made to seafarers.

Continue along the South Quay to Battery Pier and view Douglas Harbour. The pier is actually named the King Edward VIII Pier after the uncrowned English king. At the turning circle, take the road up to the Douglas Head lighthouse, which was first built in 1832, redesigned in 1859 and stands 63 feet high.

Take the steps and footpath uphill to Douglas Head, enjoying the expansive views over the town and Douglas Bay to

Heritage Pub Walks in the Isle of Man

Onchan Head and beyond, to Snaefell and other northern peaks. The open space has been a popular viewpoint and open space for decades, and in Victorian times had a cliff railway and towards the end of that era, an observation tower. Dating from Victorian times, the Great Union Camera Obscura is a different opportunity to enjoy the outstanding views on the headland. It has been restored and is open to the public, but only when there is a flag flying from its roof.

Swing round to the right away from the views of the town to enjoy views south along the coast. Soon you will enter the three mile stretch of the Marine Drive and its gateway, built in 1891 and a very popular excursion for the Victorian and Edwardian tourists. Originally there was a rail track with an electric tram to take visitors to the resort of Port Soderick down the coast. The Drive is no longer passable by car because of rock falls, but it is an excellent place to walk or cycle, taking care to keep away from either side. The views are marvellous, stretching out to Langness with its lighthouse and St Michael's Isle with its fort and chapel, as well as to the English Lakeland fells. Boats may be seen with people fishing off the Head and seabirds will circle and call above and below on the cliffs.

The pavement continues along the road the length of the Marine Drive and slightly beyond. At the T junction turn left and, after about a quarter of a mile, look for the footpath just beyond the seat on the side of the road on a bend. You will notice the grey buildings of the Port Soderick complex below. Follow the footpath signs for the coastal path to Port Soderick, taking the downward path just behind a gorse hedge then zigzagging on steps to the beach and the front at Port Soderick. In Victorian times, where the Marine Drive ends and the tramway finished, passengers took a cliff railway to

Ann Reeder

the shore, from where they would transfer to the Isle of Man Steam Railway on the Douglas Port Erin line.

Pause for a break at the beach, enjoying the views out to sea, as the Victorian tourists would have done.

Turn inland through the lower car park and enter Port Soderick Glen. Take the path on the left hand side of the stream, cross the bridge and turn right. Climb the glen, cross the stream and turn left up hill going slightly seawards briefly then curve sharply to the right. Fork right at the junction of two paths and take the steps up to the road (the handrail eases the climb). Follow the path to the road and turn left uphill towards the railway bridge about half a mile further on. Immediately after going under the bridge, turn left onto the track to the station (now a private home) and catch the steam train back to Douglas.

If the railway is not running, take the road and then a path alongside the railway for a short distance, then follow the Old Castletown Road back to Bridge Road at the Quay in Douglas, near the railway station.

Turn left out of the station at Douglas and up Athol Street before turning right into Church Street to reach the Rovers Return.

'Walk' 10 The final lap—the tour of the motorcycles and the view from the top

The Sulby Glen Hotel, the TT course and a short ascent of Snaefell

On previous walks from this book you may have visited significant parts of the Isle of Man and been captivated by its scenery and fascinated by Manx heritage. But before you leave the island, catch the spirit of the TT (Tourist Trophy motorcycle races) and take a lingering look at the beauty of Mann. On this variation of a walk, you will drive the 37.7 miles of the TT course starting at the Grandstand in Douglas. When you are over half way round, you will stop off at the Bungalow so that you can walk up to the summit of Snaefell to take a last look at the island and enjoy its diversity. From the top, weather permitting and trying to ignore the wind, you should enjoy superb views not only of the Isle of Man, but across to England, Scotland, Ireland North and South and on rare occasions, Wales—and, as some would say, Neptune and Heaven as well.

Address:	The Sulby Glen Hotel, Main Road, Sulby IM7 2HR
Tel:	01624 897240
Hours:	Daily noon until midnight
Real ale:	The pub's own beer Dunlop Draught, Bushy's, Okells and guests

Ann Reeder

Food: Daily from 12.30 pm to 2 pm and from 6 pm to 9 pm in the bar or bistro including bar meals, vegetarian, Sunday carvery and Chef's specials
Parking: Car park

The Sulby Glen Hotel and Bistro is a traditional country inn, located on one of the fastest stretches of the TT course, with views of mountains and glens. The Sulby Glen Hotel has been voted Isle of Man Breweries Pub of the Year, has twice been voted Isle of Man CAMRA pub of the year and holds the Cask Marque. Home cooked food and over 40 whiskies are available, there are pub games and occasional live music, free Wi-Fi, and accommodation.

Manx heritage

Joey Dunlop and the Manx TT

Address: The Bungalow
Hours: Daylight hours
Charge: Free
Catering: Not available
Shop: Not available
Parking: At the Bungalow

The statue at Bungalow Corner on the Mountain Road (the A18 between Ramsey and Douglas) shows TT legend Joey Dunlop on a Honda. It was made of bronze by Manx sculptor Amanda Barton. NIcknamed 'the King of the Road', Joey Dunlop (1952-2000) won a record 26 races at the TT, including hat-tricks (winning three races in a week) in 1985, 1988 and 2000. The Joey Dunlop Cup is now presented to the most successful overall rider at the TT and the area around the 26th milestone of the TT course has been renamed "Joey's".

The TT races started on the Island because road racing in Britain was forbidden by Act of Parliament and discouraged by the introduction of a 20 mph speed limit in 1903. The Isle of Man allowed temporary road closures for racing on public roads. The first race was on 28 May 1907. Initially it took a different route, but the current course, the Mountain Course, has been used since 1911. A lap is 37.73 miles, starting and finishing in Douglas, and there are at least 220 corners, numerous hairpins, roads through built-up areas and a level crossing. The current lap record of 131.578 mph was set in 2009 by John McGuinness, and riders can reach over 190 mph in places. There are vantage points and a range of entertainment alongside the TT, including motorcycle envy as bikers admire machines lined up along the Prom in Douglas and around the island!

The building behind the Joey Dunlop statue was a World War Two telecommunications headquarters and housed Murray's Motorcycle Museum until it closed in 2005.

Snaefell (Snow Mountain)

Address: Off the Mountain Road
Hours: Daylight hours and in clear weather
Charge: Free
Catering: At the Snaefell Summit Hotel/café
Shop: Gifts, postcards and souvenirs from the Snaefell Summit café
Parking: At the Bungalow before walking or taking the mountain railway

Ann Reeder

Snaefell is the island's highest mountain, reaching 2,036 feet (621 metres) above sea level. Its name comes from the Norse, meaning Snow Mountain. The summit is distinguished by the terminus of the Snaefell Mountain Railway, a café (originally a hotel) and two communications masts (that help you identify Snaefell from many parts of the island). You can see the 'three legs' of the Sulby Reservoir as well as surrounding peaks of the northern hills and to the south, beyond the Central Valley, the summits of South Barrule and Cronk-ny-Arrey-Lhaa are visible. Around you, you can see the western Scottish coastline from the Mull of Galloway to the Solway Firth, the Lakeland fells, including Scafell Pike, the highest peak in England, while towards Wales, you may see Snowdon and the Isle of Anglesey and to the west, the Irish coastline from Strangford Lough to the Mountains of Mourne.

The 'Snaefell Summit Hotel' was opened originally in 1895 when the electric railway was built from Laxey to the summit. Refurbished in winter 2010/11, it serves lunches and snacks, and has been running occasional popular sunset dinners, in conjunction with the Snaefell Mountain Railway. Telephone 01624 673631 for further details; early booking is strongly advised for the Sunset Dinners.

The walk (Medium; less than two miles; 30 minutes ascent and 20 minutes descent)

'Walk' 10
SNAEFELL

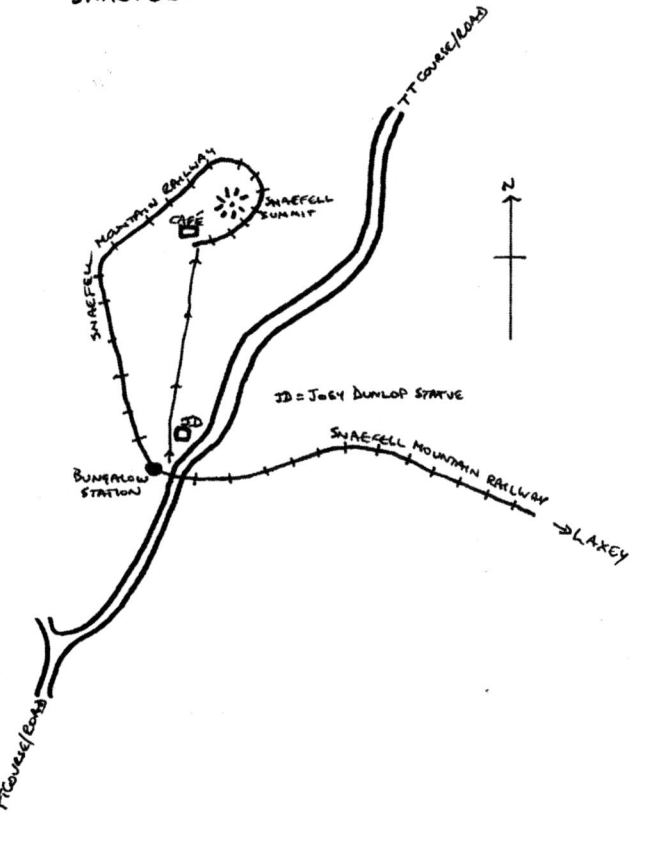

It is a steady but moderate ascent of about one mile from the Bungalow, starting at about 1,360 feet above sea level. It should take less than 30 minutes to reach the summit of Snaefell, depending on your fitness. The terrain is mostly grassy, but as it can be marshy in places, especially after rain, you should wear tough and waterproof boots. The walk is only worthwhile if the weather is clear. (There is a Snaefell Mountain Railway station at the Bungalow so you could travel up or down by train if preferred).

The drive, incorporating a real ale pub and a mountain walk (37.7 miles)

"WALK 10"
TT COURSE

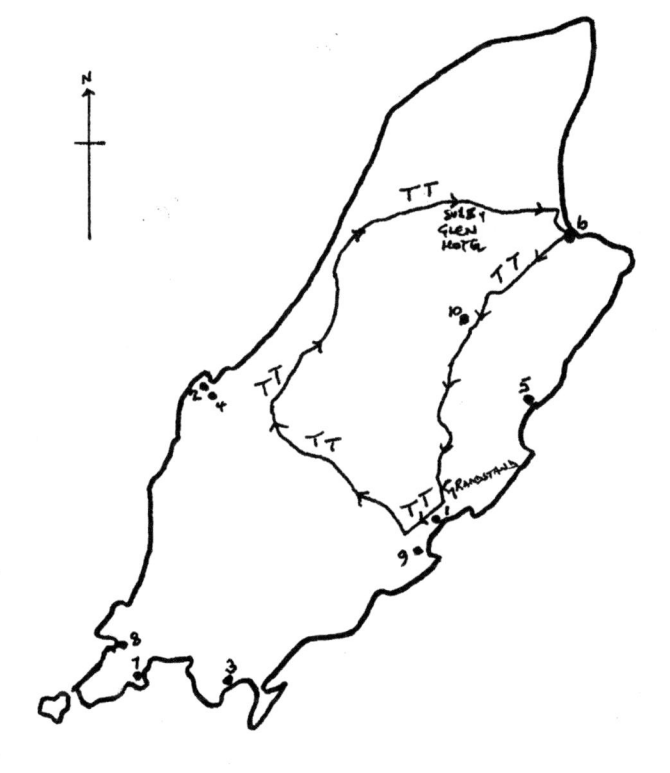

Ann Reeder

Start at the Grandstand in Douglas on Glencruthery Road, taking the clockwise direction of the course as ridden in practice week and in the week of the races in early June each year. You will notice the milestones all of the way round the course.

Pass St Andrew's Church and St Ninian's School. Keep in the right hand lane at the traffic lights at the top of Bray Hill, noticing views of Douglas Head ahead and to your left as you go down Bray Hill. Continue into Quarterbridge Road through residential streets to reach the double roundabouts at Quarterbridge.

At the first roundabout opposite the Quarterbridge pub, turn right and at the second roundabout go straight over onto Peel Road (A1). You will be above the access road that was built to help residents and visitors travel around the island during the road closures for the practices and races.

On the double bends, continue past the popular grandstand seating next to the church at Braddan Bridge, passing the second milestone as you drive uphill. Travel down through Union Mills, climb up to Glen Vine (and the fourth milestone) and through Crosby along the Central Valley to Ballacraine.

Turn right at the Ballacraine cross roads, following the road to Ramsey (A3).

Continue through Glen Helen, Cronk-y-Voddy and Kirk Michael (the 14th milestone is in the village), pass the stately Bishopscourt and continue through Ballaugh, go over the hump back bridge and pass the Curraghs Wildlife Park, after

Heritage Pub Walks in the Isle of Man

which you will reach Sulby and the 19th milestone, roughly half way round the course.

Stop off at the Sulby Glen Hotel, a regular CAMRA award winner, which is located on one of the fastest sections of the course, the Sulby Straight.

Resume the TT course (A3 still), passing the Glen Kella 'whisky' distillery and Ginger Hall and drive through Churchtown and the centre of Ramsey.

In Ramsey, at the crossroads with the town hall opposite, turn right and follow the road round. Follow the signpost for the A18 Douglas, taking a sharp left up the Hairpin, one of the slowest bends on the course. Continue the ascent out of Ramsey around the Waterworks, enjoying views of the sea over the east coast.

You will pass the 25th milestone and will be climbing on the Mountain Road. Gooseneck Corner is one of many popular viewing spots as it is a slow 'right hander uphill'. As you are not racing, you can pause to enjoy the views 'down the north' to the Point of Ayre lighthouse and to Scotland beyond. You can see Albert Tower on your right and the summit of North Barrule on your left.

As you round the Verandah bends, you will get a view of the Laxey Wheel in the distance ahead and the track of the Snaefell Mountain Railway down to the left and up to the right.

Your next stop will be the Bungalow Bridge, another major viewpoint after the mountain climb. The mountain railway crosses here and stops to collect or set down passengers. You are immediately below the highest mountain on the island, Snaefell, and can choose whether to walk up it or take the train. There is a car park here, and the impressive statue of the late TT legend, Joey Dunlop.

Having visited Snaefell and admired the statue, resume your TT journey on the A18 towards Douglas on the Mountain Road and through the northern hills. After the 31st milestone, you will go through Brandywell, the highest point on the course. You will have glimpses of the coast and of the Baldwin Valleys through which the Millennium Way passes.

Drive straight down towards Douglas, passing Katie's Cottage and enjoying a patchwork of fields towards the Central Valley. At a sharp right hand bend, you will pass the grandstand seating at Creg-ny-Baa, go through Brandish Corner and reach the outskirts of Douglas.

A left hand bend at Hillberry takes you to Signpost Corner and a right hander at a roundabout, where you turn right, signed Douglas. Governors Bridge takes you off course as a car driver; the motorcyclists actually loop down the 'dip' on the old road. You have to turn right at the mini roundabout, towards Douglas on the A2 and over another mini roundabout (where riders emerge from the 'dip') to rejoin Glencruthery Road.

As you pass the rugby club and police headquarters you are approaching the Grandstand, the giant scoreboard, the Pits and the finishing line in Douglas.

You will have done the full 37.7 miles of the TT course. Calculate the time it took you and compare it with the fastest times done by motorcyclists on the course—regularly less than 18 minutes!

The route will have given you an interesting experience as well as wonderful views of the island in all its beautiful diversity, from the roads and from the summit of Snaefell.

Useful contacts and information

Isle of Man Tourism
Web: www.visitisleofman.com
Tel: 01624 686766
Visit: The Welcome Centre in the Sea Terminal Building in Douglas is open seven days a week from 8 am to 6 pm

Manx National Heritage (including the Story of Mann)
Web: www.gov.im/mnh
Tel: 01624 648000

Isle of Man Transport
Web: www.iombusandrail.info/
Buses: 01624 662525
Railways: 01624 663366
Horse Trams: 01624 696420

Warning: If you arrive by car or hire one, pick up a parking disc on arrival at the Welcome Centre or airport information desk. You will need it for free parking; use the clock on the disc to point to the time you parked the car.

Weather
Ronaldsway Meteorological Office
Personalised weather forecast service 0900 6243 200
Weather forecast 0900 6243 300

Consideration while walking in the country

- Respect the life of the countryside
- Protect wildlife, wild plants and trees
- Keep to the paths across farmland
- Fasten all gates
- Avoid damaging fences, hedges, styles and walls
- Leave no litter—take it home
- Keep dogs under proper control and clear up after them
- Guard against all risk of fire
- Safeguard water supplies and do not pollute them
- Go carefully on country roads

Take sensible precautions in the event of the weather changing, wear strong shoes or boots, carry a rainproof jacket, map and compass, and check the weather before you go off the beaten track. If you walk with a dog, please use the green bins provided on many footpaths on the island.

About the author

Country walker Ann Reeder has been visiting the Isle of Man regularly since 1986, particularly to enjoy the coastal scenery, hill walks and heritage. She has introduced a number of tour groups to the island. She is a member of CAMRA.